In

satori ananda – awaken to happiness

"A true gentleman emerges through sharing his deepest fears and insecurities. Michael Tranmer knows how to peel back the layers of self-deception and see beyond the surface into the root of the masculine armor. By fearlessly sharing his personal transformation story in *satori ananda,* he reveals a big heart that just wants to be loved."
— Shamen Durek, International Bestselling Author of *Spirit Hacking*

"I read *satori ananda* in one day—I literally could not put it down. Michael Tranmer has given us a beautifully authentic and raw look into the journey we go through in loss and in rediscovering who we really are in that process. This is a must-read for anyone who is going through challenging times or a big transition as it provides not only a compelling story we can all relate to, it also guides you to uncovering your own truth and next steps in the journey of life and love."
— Karen McGregor, International Speaker and Bestselling Author of *The Tao of Influence,* Founder of Speaker Success Formula

"You won't be able to put it down. A powerfully vulnerable, entertaining and uplifting book about one man's journey from marriage breakdown to awakening to consciousness. This raw, honest and truly joyful book will take you on a journey you won't soon forget."
— Teresa de Grosbois, Founder of the Evolutionary Business Council, #1 International Bestselling Author of *Mass Influence*

"It's rare that any 21st Century man would share his personal journey of pain that led him to his own personal enlightenment. Bravo, to Michael Tranmer's courage to take us on his intimate journey to the inner workings of his wounded heart. As Rumi so eloquently stated, 'the wound is where the light gets in.' In the end, it's all about self-love radiating out from your heart to a partner and then to the world. Love is the most complex and exhilarating feeling on Earth. To learn and express the tragedies and triumphs in such exquisite detail is another matter; *satori ananda* has both."

– Gary Stuart, three-time Bestselling Author and Master Constellation Facilitator

"In *satori ananda* we witness the emergence of the Divine Masculine, self-reflective with emotional capacity. Michael Tranmer beautifully illustrates the journey to presence and love after being cracked open with pain. When tough stuff happens, we can either wall it off and go numb, or we can be courageous enough to feel the vulnerability of the human experience. Bravo Michael, for your raw unfolding into inner discovery, and willingness to pave the way for the masculine to reclaim its heart."

– Kerri Hummingbird, International Bestselling Author of
The Second Wave: Transcending the Human Drama

"Raw, vulnerable, tender, courageous. Michael Tranmer's *satori ananda* is all this and more. As this memoir takes you on his journey through dynamic life changes, huge uncertainties and deep personal reflection, you are transported into his transformational awakening experience. Make this beautiful introduction to mindfulness and spirituality a companion on your own journey to happiness and fulfillment."

– Valerie René Sheppard, Self-Mastery Counselor and
Multi-Award-Winning Author of *Living Happy to Be ME!*©

"Michael Tranmer has a powerful way of capturing heartbreak. His description of his emotional and spiritual journey captured my attention from the start. His beautiful way with words reminds us that we are all human beings navigating complex emotions. I can't recommend this book enough to show readers comfort about being in a tough spot and hope that the journey forward is around the corner."

– Kara Deringer, three-time International Bestselling Author,
International Speaker, University Instructor

"From the first page, the intense introspection in *satori ananda* will have you moving through a delicate dance of emotions ranging from sadness to joy. Michael Tranmer unabashedly shares the lessons learned after hitting his rock bottom, a journey that is both heartbreaking and uplifting. An inspiring read to gain hard-earned wisdom without enduring similar pain."
– Sharon Sayler, International Bestselling Author, Host of the #1 show on OMTimes Radio *"The Autoimmune Hour"*

"Michael Tranmer has genuinely woven a captivating story about his personal transformation. He is unquestionably an eloquent writer with a unique skill for painting beautiful imagery with his words. I didn't just read *satori ananda,* I felt like I lived it. With each sentence I was drawn in for the next revelation, emotion and perfectly placed morsel of wisdom. As a Transformational Coach, I kept thinking of a few of my personal clients who will benefit from reading this book. If you're ready to escape to beautiful locations while unearthing more in your life, *satori ananda* is the book for you."
– P.J. Dixon, Award-Winning International Speaker and Transformation Coach, and Author

"While some books share stories, powerful journeys, and transformations, others are more 'how-to': offering perspectives & approaches that support living a happier and more fulfilled life. *satori ananda* offers a nice balance of both. Tranmer reminds his reader that gentle, mental discipline (plus curiosity to learn new things) is a great combination for waking up to who you truly are."
– Ben Gioia, two-time Bestselling Author

"*satori ananda* is one man's story of stepping into the light, to rediscover, to remember and to live the truth of who he is. Vulnerable and true, it's easy to feel how this could be Everyman's story."
– Laurie Seymour, two-time #1 Bestselling Author, Host of the WisdomTalk Radio Podcast, Executive Coach, International Speaker and Founder/CEO of The Baca Institute

"Michael Tranmer shows how vulnerability is a strength—not a weakness—as he rebuilds himself following his separation. A true, inspirational story that will have you asking yourself what else is possible for your own life. A courageous journey of transformation, I loved it."

– Jean Kay, Poet, Songwriter, Professional Member of the
Canadian Author's Association

"Beautifully and eloquently written. *satori ananda* is a timeless story of the human heart. Tranmer takes you on an exquisite journey of awakening and self discovery."

– Lee-Ann Frances Bates, Bestselling Author, Experiential Transformation
Facilitator, International Speaker and Coach

"*satori ananda* is one of the most powerful books I've ever experienced. From the very first page, Michael Tranmer sweeps you off your feet, takes hold of your heart, and guides you on a journey of deep emotional & spiritual healing. A brilliant writer and masterful teacher, Michael courageously shares his real-world insights through a lens of honest vulnerability and naked authenticity. If you are struggling with loss or heartache—or find yourself at a crossroads—these inspiring pages will help you rise from the ashes with the strength, courage & clarity to live your best life."

– davidji, Author of Nautilus Gold Medal Winner *Sacred Powers, #1*
Bestselling *Destressifying*, Award-Winning *Secrets of Meditation*

SATORI
ANANDA

awaken to
happiness

Keep shining
your brilliant light.

SATORI ANANDA

awaken to happiness

A TRANSFORMATIONAL MEMOIR BY

MICHAEL C.W. TRANMER

PROMINENCE PUBLISHING

MICHAEL C. W. TRANMER
satori ananda — awaken to happiness

Copyright © 2020 by Michael C. W. Tranmer
First edition

ISBN: 978-1-988925-63-9

For further information on corporate speaking engagements, live book performances and for social media links to past talks, please connect with Michael through his website: **michaeltranmer.com**

Cover & interior design by Laura Wrubleski
Author photo by Ryan Deasley
Published by Prominence Publishing **prominencepublishing.com**

Typeset in Garamond Premier Pro

To all the darkened souls,
let this book be your light.

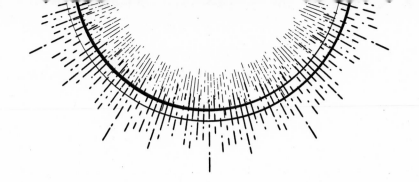

CONTENTS

SATORI
ANANDA

awaken to happiness

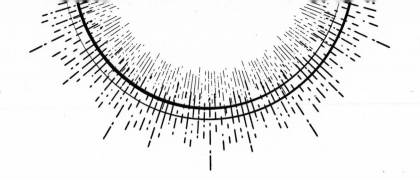

CHAPTER 1

AWAKENING

*The awakening of consciousness is the
next evolutionary step for mankind.*

ECKHART TOLLE

The view was magnificent from the faded brown chaise in our
Vancouver condo. The towers in Yaletown, on the other side of
False Creek, looked close enough to touch. The peaks of the North
Shore mountains, beyond the towers, gave a natural frame for the city
below. But on that day, instead of admiring the view, my wife and I
sat facing the opposite direction. We stole the occasional glimpse into
each other's eyes, to see the tears streaming down, as we discussed the
end of our marriage.

I absorbed blow after blow, as she detailed why she was no longer
getting what she needed from our life together. My heart cracked as she

delivered a list of times when I disappointed her: the time in Australia, when I snuck away from the animal sanctuary in boredom and left her on her own; the time when I didn't pick her up at her parents, after her long day of wedding dress shopping; the time I refused to consider her brother as a groomsman in our wedding. With each example I crumbled into smaller pieces.

My mind raced trying to figure out why she hadn't said something sooner. But even if she had, I wondered if it would have mattered, and if I would have behaved differently. In that moment it didn't make a difference, I was disappointed in myself. That behaviour did not reflect the type of person I wanted to be.

With the final blow, "I am not in love with you anymore," a deep moan rose from the abyss of my shattered soul. Then the realization, I had heard this noise before. This noise was the same deep, sobbing moan, that came from the bathroom of my childhood home when my parents were divorcing. This noise also came from my mother. Every night Mom would turn on the bathtub faucets with hopes of drowning out the noise. It never worked. The deep guttural moan would travel through the top floor of our home, into the bedrooms where my sisters and I were pretending to sleep. We never spoke of the nightly crying, even though it went on for months. We never thought to ask if she was okay. We never really talked about the divorce; we didn't know how.

Just as fast as the first realization came, a second arrived: my inability to effectively communicate contributed to the downfall of our marriage. What was supposed to be the perfect fairy tale marriage, was now headed towards a painful end. We had the perfect Whistler wedding, Maui honeymoon, the stable life in the city. Each of us had professional jobs, we had a condo to call home, we had shared dreams of a life and family together. But somehow along the way the dreams changed, we grew apart and neither of us realized it until it was too late.

With nothing left to say, I found the strength to retreat to the bedroom, to process what had just happened. My wife stayed in the living room and began to make up a bed on the chaise. With so many thoughts swirling through my mind, I tried to make sense of it all. I must learn from this, I thought; I must grow from this experience. I had to do everything in my power to never again feel this crushing pain in my heart. I remembered I had a journal—a long-forgotten gift from my father. It was stashed away somewhere in my closet. Going to the closet, I dug through the shelves until I found it.

Opening to the first blank page I started to write. I wrote about the conversation that had just happened, and about the events over the past few months that led up to it. I wrote what I was feeling, what I was thinking. I wrote about all the thoughts passing through my confused mind. It was my first time journaling. As an egoic thirty-six-year-old male, writing about intense emotional pain was never something I had explored. Writing everything down helped get the thoughts out of my head and onto paper, where I could begin to process it all.

I wrote about our lack of communication, about developing different dreams, all of which helped to explain the distance that had grown between us. The unhappy trips we had recently taken which were all so awkward and unexplainable at the time, now made perfect sense. While I thought we were just going through a funk, it was now obvious that she had been getting clear on the future that she wanted—a future that didn't include me. The connection that we first made twelve years ago, back in 2005, was now forever lost. The final realization of the prospect of a lonely life haunted me as I attempted sleep for the night.

The moment I opened my eyes the next morning I felt a wave of sadness. I was alone. Lying there I wondered, if it's just me, then what was the point of getting out of bed? What was the point of going to work? What future was I working towards? Until the previous day, every moment, every thought, every decision, was for us as a couple. Without her, what was the point? Staring at the bedroom ceiling, I knew that feeling of loneliness was going to be my biggest battle to overcome. The grief was so heavy; I had no idea how I was going to move forward.

I rubbed my eyes and the time on the bedside alarm clock came into focus. In that moment I became painfully aware that this was actually happening: I was waking to the end of our marriage. All the plans and visions for our life together, the kids we were going to have, the full house of love and laughter, the stupid white picket fence, the growing old together, all of it had vanished. The thought made me shudder and release the first of many tears that day. Tears that would become my new companion in the months that followed.

I lingered in bed under the weight of my broken heart. I attempted to find something to motivate me to get out of bed. Eventually my mind drifted to a painting that I had always liked and wanted to buy. A painting that showcased the power of the mountains that I loved so much. A painting I never bought because the wall for which it was destined was to remain empty and not clutter the small condo, according to my wife. A painting that, in that moment, I decided I was going to buy and hang where I pleased. With that one thought of inspiration I slowly crawled out of bed to face the day and my new reality. I had lost the person that I loved. When I lost her and our love died, the person I was when I was with her also died. I couldn't know it at the time, but something new—a new version of me—would emerge out of the loss.

A day later I faced a long weekend alone with only my troubled head. That morning my wife of six years, partner for twelve, had moved out of our place and in with her parents. I knew I needed to make some plans and get out of the condo. I texted a friend, who instantly replied, "Yes, of course I can meet you." Jessie was one of my oldest friends and happened to be visiting Vancouver that weekend. We had known each other since kindergarten back in Kingston, Ontario, where we both grew up. The fact that she was in town, when I needed her the most, was the first of many miracles the Universe would offer over the coming months.

I left the condo with my headphones on and my hood up, ready to embrace the miserable November rains. Vancouver, like the rest of the Pacific Northwest, endures a long, dark winter with frequent rain. While the rain keeps the forests green and puts snow on the hills, the lack of sun could be challenging for my mental state. As I walked, I became aware of how nervous I was to see Jessie and explain my situation. Each block I wiped away tears that mixed with raindrops falling on my face.

Twenty minutes later I walked into the restaurant on Fourth Avenue in Kitsilano. It was well ahead of the dinner rush so there were plenty of tables available. I spotted Jessie at a corner table along the back wall. The restaurant was dark, furnished with thick wood. Heavy, moody music filled the space. It was a perfect setting to match my sombre mood. We settled in at our table. It took only minutes before we were both in tears.

I walked her through what I knew, for her benefit as much as for mine. As I told Jessie the details about the sudden separation, she listened without judgment or anger. She felt my words with understanding, compassion, and warmth. She respected boundaries and asked all the right questions. She helped us both try to understand how this could have happened. With hands held across the table, she helped me release wave after wave of heavy emotions that rose to the surface.

"You should eat," said Jessie. She was right, and I appreciated her being straightforward with me, as she always had been. While we lived in opposite corners of the country, we had managed to stay in touch over the years. So much had happened in both our lives during that time, but we were always there for each other. She could sense that I had been struggling with organizing and consuming food in recent days. Food had been the last thing on my mind.

Once the food arrived, we continued to talk. "Do you remember what I said to you, when you were in Vancouver earlier in the year?" I asked, part way through our dinner.

"No, what was that?" she said.

"I said I had this feeling. That something was going to happen. Things seemed to be going so well for all our friends. I had this feeling that something bad was coming. At the time, I thought it was going to be an illness, or death, and I never thought *it* would happen to me."

"Yeah, I remember that conversation."

What I didn't tell her in that moment, was that subconsciously I had been waiting for years for something to happen. I always had this underlying desire for something to occur, that would shake up my predictable world. I thought that perhaps an earthquake or some other natural disaster would cause a disruption in my repetitive eat-sleep-work routine. In that moment it became clear, with the implosion of my marriage, I had gotten what I had wished for.

Eventually we finished the meal and left the restaurant. When I checked my phone once outside, I realized we had spent almost three hours completely present with each other. It was a new experience for me; lengthy meals with enriched conversations were never a part of my past. Before that night, most restaurant meals with friends were spent staring at a hockey game on a nearby TV. Connection was only made through the passing of a pitcher of beer. Not exactly deep and soulful experiences. Later I realized that this lack of connection had nothing to do with beer or hockey games. Instead it had to do with me: my insecurities and inability to vulnerably open my heart and connect with others. Like she had countless times before, Jessie had been there to help me move forward.

———————

Later that weekend I headed back to the same restaurant chain, this time at the Main Street location. The setting was the same: the same tear-filled walk in the rain, the same dark decor, the same sad music. All of it seemed to fuel the turbulent emotions pulsing through my body. After I entered the restaurant, I found two seats at the bar and got ready for another marathon dinner, this time with my friend Ash. Once she arrived, we both ordered drinks and settled into our seats.

Ash and I had been friends for many years in Vancouver. We had first met when she was dating a buddy of mine. We had shared numerous ski, surf and bike adventures over the years. We had endured many challenging times in the mountains and in the ocean but sharing emotional trauma was a first.

After I brought Ash up to date on my breakup, she started to talk about her personal relationships, her greatest fears, and her deepest insecurities. I realized that by opening up about my separation, she also felt comfortable sharing about her life. Both painful and therapeutic, this vulnerability led to a deeper trust and connection between us. The

sharing helped with the healing. Ironically, this capacity for meaningful connection was one of the things missing from my marriage. I wondered if the lack of connection in the marriage stemmed from a level of
trust that was never really there.

Sitting with Ash, I questioned whether I was just trying to prove
that I could listen, connect, and converse at a higher level. Was I working on these new skills with hopes of getting back together with my
wife? So many thoughts swirled in my head throughout our dinner—
so many, that I started to make a list of notes on a napkin. I didn't want
to lose track of the questions that required further thought. I had no
idea where the thoughts would take me, but I knew I had to explore
deeper. This new life of looking inward and dissecting my thoughts was
here to stay.

"You should write about what's going on with me," I pleaded with
Ash, who was a journalist. She had the skills to capture in words what
was pulsing through my brain. Surely, she could clearly articulate these
new thoughts, these new feelings, the depth of these new emotions
that had awakened inside me. Surely, she could make the clear contrast
between the old, reserved, quiet me, with this new me that was emerging. She politely declined the request, while giving a look of empathy.

"You are special, you know that, right?" she said, changing the sub-
ject. I could only reply with more tears; I was a mess. In the span of only
a few days my wife had left me and, in her place, there had entered a
new level of awareness that was revealing some unsavoury truths about
myself, and my personality. In full body sobs, I put my head down on
the bar in the middle of the busy restaurant.

"If I am so special, then how did I end up in this world of hurt?" I
asked, not expecting a reply.

This living at emotional extremes was so new to me. It was hard, heavy, and exhausting. At the same time, I wanted to go deeper to try and better understand all that I was thinking, all that I was feeling. As hard as it was, I couldn't ignore what was coming to the surface. Over the course of our dinner I filled the remaining space on my napkin with more thoughts and resources from Ash, to help get me through the upcoming week.

Back outside after dinner I gave Ash a long hug goodbye. Under a dark sky of endless rain, I once again put my hood up, my headphones on, and started what was becoming a regular tear-filled walk back to my empty condo. The residential streets were mostly vacant, the sidewalks covered with a wet mat of fallen leaves. As I trudged through the darkness my mind drifted to all the texts, calls, and now meals with friends, I had had since the separation. Even though less than a week had passed, I felt exhausted trying to process all the pain, while trying to understand how this could have happened. But as I got closer to the condo, I started to appreciate how fortunate I was to have these people in my life. To have friends that cared, friends that were sending me love. They had always been there for me, but in that moment, I began to value them at a whole new level.

Once inside, I used the energy from this gratitude to make my way to bed for another night of restless sleep.

I awoke early the next morning and watched a video online from a local radio host named Stacey. In the video I noticed that she had been walking down the same street, Broadway Avenue, that I had been on the night before. The text across the video read: "to all the crying people in the streets tonight, I see you". I was floored. My first tears of the new day arrived with the synchronicity of Stacey's post. While I knew we did not directly pass each other, I was in awe at the timing and the depth of her message.

Without hesitation, I replied to her post and messaged her. "Thank you, I've cried on every sidewalk I've been on this week," I wrote.

"Oh ya, sure ya have," she replied.

Her guarded reply was expected, considering her public profile and the likely volume of less than sincere messages she received. It took a few exchanges of messages, but eventually I convinced her that I was being authentic.

"Thank you for seeing me, and for seeing others," I typed towards the end of our exchange.

The rawness of this and her other posts resonated with me because of her uncensored vulnerability. She helped others by being her true self and sharing the emotional struggles that others suppressed. I vowed to one day meet Stacey and thank her in person.

As I was still lying in bed, my phone vibrated with the day's first text message. It was from a friend in Toronto, just checking in on me. The text brought the next wave of sorrow to the day. I knew my friend's life wasn't perfect, but in that moment, I would have traded him in a heartbeat. I envisioned his life full of love, with a devoted wife and two kids they adored. It was the life I wanted, the life I was working towards, the life that, to some extent, had been stolen from me. Instead, all I had was a pounding headache from too many drinks at dinner with Ash the night before. I put the phone down on the bedside table and lay back to stare at the ceiling.

"Breathe, Mike," I said to myself. It was all I could do in that moment.

———

Later in the week I headed to the local kickboxing studio for some much-needed exercise. Halfway through the class, punching with the strength of all my demons, my emotions began to rise to the surface. How could this separation have happened? Was there anything I could have done? Why didn't she give me more of a chance? These thoughts bounced around in my head as I punished the punching bag in a relentless attack. Each blow unleashed more anger, frustration, and sadness. As the exercises reached a climax, I had to do everything possible to prevent bursting into tears in front of twenty strangers.

I quickly changed my clothes after the class. I dashed out the front door with my backpack just before the pain took over and the tears rushed out. Coming out of the studio I headed south towards West 7th Avenue. At the intersection I was faced with a seemingly simple choice: left, or right? Left, I could go straight back to the sadness, loneliness, and pain-filled familiar condo. Or right, I could take my first steps away from my old life and begin to explore a new world. In that moment it seemed as though the choice was far from simple: it was a decision about finding the courage to accept the reality of my new life. Staring up into the dark night sky and the perpetual cold drizzling rain, I put my hood up, my headphones on, and took my first steps to the right, towards my new life.

A block later I turned left on to Fir Street and was once again overcome with deep, full-body sobs. The pain of the swirling emotions was too much to contain. Without a planned destination I continued to walk with my head low, to hide my tears. Under the edge of my hood I could barely see the footsteps of an approaching couple. As they got closer, I heard their conversation before I saw their faces. "Will it look good next to the couch?" the woman asked the man, referring to a new table for their living room. I used to have conversations like that, I thought. They were conversations that I missed. At the same time, I wondered how the couple connected on a deeper level. That deeper connection my wife and I once had, but somehow lost along the way. The connection that I craved to have once again. They didn't notice me as we passed, and we continued our different journeys.

Two blocks later the sobbing subsided. The weight of the fear that accompanied each step into an unknown future was replaced with a moment of clarity. In that moment, I fully realized the extent of the trauma I absorbed when my wife spoke those eight words: "I am no longer in love with you." With those words, the bridge to a defined future was severed in half. All plans, all visions, gone. Hearing her speak those words felt like a screw was being twisted deep through the core of my soul.

Before the thought escaped my mind, I hurried to find a place to record it in my journal, which I carried in my backpack. Writing the words helped make real the extremes of the emotions I was processing. Relieved that the thought was out of my head and recorded in the journal, I took a deep breath and looked skyward before placing the journal back in my bag and continuing my walk.

I started to feel better as the wave of emotion from the realization passed. As I continued up Fir Street the rain eased to a mist, as my tears did the same. I removed my hood, wiped my eyes, and prepared to meet the gaze of passing strangers. I walked into an unlit park and noticed the scent of the wet fallen leaves. The darkness; the lightly misting rain; the heaviness of wet leaves, I felt like I was walking in a moody movie scene, perfectly matched to my emotions. I walked farther into the unlit park and took a series of deep breaths to let go of the final remnants of pain I had been carrying. With my emotions in check, I turned my attention to my other major challenge: my severely neglected stomach—I needed to eat.

I left the park and walked towards Granville Street. Crossing at the lights I took a right turn towards a jazz bar. I studied the menu posted outside, then took a long gaze through the front door. The space was full of happy couples and larger groups. Everyone was smiling and laughing under the glow of bright lights. The sound of up-beat jazz from the live band filled the bar. This would not do.

I took another deep breath; I would not give up. Turning north down Granville, I crossed the street and headed towards a familiar place from the past: Barney's. When my wife and I first moved to Vancouver, we lived in an apartment across the street from this neighbourhood pub. We would often meet friends at Barney's for Sunday brunch. Again, I looked inside to study the vibe before walking in. To the right of the front door was a small but busy bar. The lights were low, and a DJ played from a small space beside the bar. The barman caught my gaze and sent back a welcoming nod. With another deep breath, I pulled open the front door and stepped inside. It was going to take some time before I got used to dining alone.

I decided on an empty seat at the far corner of the bar. A wall of alcohol was straight ahead, and a TV flickered, off to the right. Both would provide something to stare at, a distraction from my loneliness. The couple to my right sat with closed shoulders, busy on their phones. They didn't notice me as I sat down. The couple to my left appeared warm, present, and engaged in real conversation.

Sitting between the two couples I became painfully aware of how alone I was. Not just alone sitting at the bar, but in life. No one was waiting at home, wondering where I was. No one was coming to join me for dinner. No one was going to help me figure out how to move forward in this new world. I took yet another deep breath; beer would help me get through this.

"How are you?" asked the bartender.

"Not good," I replied.

"Oh, I see," he answered.

"When does Happy Hour start?" asked the woman to my left, saving the awkward moment.

"Ah, well, it's close enough!" said the bartender, before introducing himself as Simon.

As the beer arrived, I took my first sip and thought that maybe I could get through this meal; maybe I could figure out a way to get through this pain. With no one to talk to, I reached into my bag and pulled out my journal. After placing it on the bar I opened the journal to the next blank page and began to record my latest thoughts on the evening.

"All right, out with it," interrupted the woman to my left.

"Um, excuse me?" I said.

"The journal, what are you writing in there? My name is Kelsey, by the way. This is my boyfriend, Jeff," she said, as Jeff reached across and shook my hand.

Slowly I offered enough of my story so Kelsey and Jeff could share in my struggle. This felt good, I thought to myself. It felt good to talk to strangers, to tell my story, to connect with them on a meaningful level. I always knew this world was out there. A world where connections could be made with caring strangers. But I never saw it; I didn't know how to get there. On top of that, I never had the courage to find it. I was too comfortable in my own self-absorbed life.

Jeff understood me, as I expressed these new feelings. He went on to share how he went through his own transformation a decade ago in his twenties. I told him how impressed I was that he knew at such a young age that there was more to this life.

"Was it a complete waste of time, my narrow mindset all these years?" I asked him.

"Not at all, my man. Everything happens at the perfect time, for the perfect reason. All your experiences to this point in your life have had meaning. Same with all the thoughts that accompanied those experiences. You weren't ready for a transformation before, now you are." I didn't say anything to him, but I had my doubts as to whether I was ready for anything.

"You're coming back to our place! You must meet our friend!" demanded Kelsey later in the night.

"But, but it's a Wednesday," I replied, and immediately became aware of the lameness of my response.

"On second thought, let's do it," I corrected myself, as we paid our bills and headed for the door.

Soon after making the short five-minute walk to Jeff and Kelsey's apartment, their friend Azalea arrived. Azalea carried her tiny, dying dog cradled in her arms. Her sick dog, which she held with love, was wrapped in a blue blanket. She said her connection with her dog was stronger than what she had with most humans. In that moment I listened intently and understood her words. For the first time in my life, I could fully appreciate the love that she felt towards her small dog. It was as though feeling the depths of my own pain had created an opening to feel the pain that others felt. I was starting to understand empathy.

What was I becoming? I wondered. What was this transformation in my thinking? A month earlier I would have thought Azalea was nuts for being so sad over a dog. I would have dismissed her as weak; I would have told her to suck it up. Instead, a gap was emerging between what I was observing and the words I replied with—if I even replied at all. Several times throughout the night I simply listened to the pain the others shared. Instead of offering my opinion, or rushing to offer a solution, I remained silent. By doing so, I allowed the others to be heard. This space, this presence, was powerful. The transformation in my thinking and in my awareness was so new to me. It was so different than how I had operated in the past. On top of everything else I was feeling, it was a lot to process. Despite that, I knew I was never going back to my old, closed state of mind.

Later in the night I received hugs from all three strangers-turned-friends, as I made my way towards the apartment door. In a brief period, all three had opened up with me about their personal struggles. But something greater occurred in their apartment that evening. By trusting me into their circle, they taught me how to listen on a deeper level; how to connect. By being vulnerable in our sharing—which started with me sharing the contents of my journal several hours earlier—we were able to skip the small talk and connect over things that mattered. They were my three angels of the night, guiding me on my journey. I was deeply grateful.

As I headed home, I reflected on my experiences over the course of the evening. The change in emotions from the start of the night to the end was so immense. At the beginning of the night I was in so much pain as I left the kickboxing class. By the end of the night I was grateful for my new friends; for a whole new experience. It turned out the world of deeper connections, that I had subconsciously craved for years, existed in the very neighbourhood I had lived in for years. Thinking further, I realized it was the connections, not the kickboxing or the alcohol, that ultimately changed my state from hurt and despair to a glimpse of hope and joy. It was a beautiful, exhausting, and intense evening.

Once home and in bed, sleep eventually arrived. I awoke the next morning, only a few hours later, to a racing mind of fears, insecurities, and doubts. Am I going manic? I wondered. I knew I needed to take better care of myself. Since the separation I had barely eaten, the focus to organize food just wasn't there. My regular sleep had been cut in half. Now I was out drinking until the early hours of the morning in the middle of the week. Maybe I wasn't achieving new clarity after all, maybe I was just undernourished, tired and drunk—a far cry from enlightenment. But still, the level of self-reflection was like nothing I had ever experienced before. It was all so new. I was so confused. Lying in bed, staring at the ceiling, I made a mental note to see a counselor as soon as possible. I needed to find out what was going on with me.

Still in bed, a pounding headache started to take hold as my phone lit up with a text. It was from my wife. Reading through I could tell that she too was in a rough mental state. In her lengthy message she attempted to explain why she chose to leave, how hard it was for her, and how horrible she felt about the whole situation. She talked about how I couldn't give her the connection that she needed, that she wanted. The pounding in my head increased in intensity as I read to the end of her note.

I put the phone down when I finished reading. I couldn't even consider piecing together a reply. Instead, the tears came fast and heavy as the irony of the situation became clear: she was the catalyst for my awakening. An awakening to a new me, capable of deep connection, presence, and awareness—the exact type of partner that she wanted, in place of the old me. It was yet another painful realization that I had long been blind to. My awakening journey had only just begun. There was no turning back from discovering further hard truths about myself.

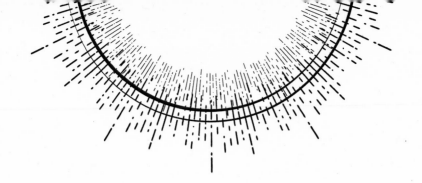

CHAPTER 2

SELF-SERVING

*When we quit thinking primarily about ourselves
and our own self-preservation, we undergo a truly
heroic transformation of consciousness.*

JOSEPH CAMPBELL

decided to take Friday off from work. Considering all that had happened over the past week, my body and my mind needed the extra break. On top of everything that was going on in my personal life, work was getting busy, with two projects heading into construction. I lingered in bed as my anxiety rose with thoughts of work.

At work, I was an engineering project manager. It was my role to coordinate teams to ensure both projects were fully designed in time for winter construction. The complexity of coordinating a multidisciplinary team of coastal engineers, geotechnical engineers as well as biologists, was beginning to wear me down. The added pressure of a demanding client, with tight deadlines, added to my stress.

For years, I struggled as an engineer. Following the footsteps of my father, and grandfather, I chose the profession for no better reason than I was good at math and science, plus it was challenging. While my father got out early and pursued law, I thought combining my love of the ocean with a specialization in coastal engineering would lead to a fulfilling career. So far, it had not. Designing structures to withstand the ocean's waves was not the same as playing in the actual waves. For over a decade I had put on my corporate mask and tried harder and harder to find meaning in my work. Lying in bed, I wondered if perhaps my efforts to find my fulfillment had been misguided.

I had slowly begun to peel this mask away in the previous years, and even more so in the short time since the separation. It was as though I no longer had to play the role of conservative engineer for fear of upsetting others, or worse, losing my job. I had so far survived my worst nightmare at home, which I translated into the ability to survive anything. I had started to be more myself in the workplace. I was speaking up more, I was sharing more of my ideas, I was tolerating less small talk. Surprisingly, that hadn't led to getting fired, but instead created a positive change around the office. My team's morale was high, my clients were happy, and my boss was giving me good feedback. If they only knew what was really going on with me. But it was too soon to share my personal life changes around the office. I decided to keep my two worlds separate, for now.

I started my day off with a return to the kick-boxing studio. My plans were derailed when I arrived to find the doors locked and the studio empty. Checking my phone, I realized I booked a class for a different day at a different studio. How did this happen? I thought. This was not me; I did not make mistakes like this. Thoughts started racing through my head that my new *state*, combined with a lack of sleep and food, was causing me to lose the sharpness that I valued so much. While my left-brained thinking hadn't yet led me to career fulfillment, I still took pride in complex problem solving and keeping my life tightly organized, like a proper engineer. A wave of fear trembled through me. Would I have to sacrifice this sharpness in exchange for my new level of awareness? Why couldn't I have both? I wondered. I took a moment as I stood outside the locked doors of the studio and reminded myself about the appointment I had booked with a counselor later that day. I took a deep breath and sighed. Hopefully he could help provide some answers to my looming questions.

Fortunately, the kick-boxing studio was located only a few minutes from the seawall in False Creek. Since I was already in my workout clothes, I decided to run the long way home along the seawall to blow off some steam. I had to take my mind off the disappointment of the morning, and the hurt of the last week. My first few steps were sluggish, and I regretted my ambitious route. But soon my pace quickened as my mind began to clear. As I ran, I began to focus all my attention on the nature that surrounded me. The wind dancing through the leaves in the trees, the glistening of the waves in False Creek, the brilliant green grass; I soaked in all the radiant vibrancy. By becoming fully present I was able to observe nature on a level I had never accessed before. As I arrived back at the condo my thoughts drifted to the two backcountry ski trips booked for the winter. The possibility of connecting deeply with nature on those trips gave me something to look forward to.

After a long shower I set out to my first appointment of the day at the local art gallery. I had been studying the online image of the painting I liked, ever since that first morning after the separation. Today was the day I would finally get to see it in person. On my way out of the condo I bumped into my neighbour. We started to walk together as we were both heading towards Granville Island. For the first time in over a decade, we engaged in a real conversation—on something other than the weather. After a couple of blocks, I learned that she was an avid music fan who traveled all over North America to take in live shows. Before we went our separate ways, I was amazed when she offered me a ticket to an upcoming show in Vancouver for one of my new favourite bands, The National.

Since being introduced to the band around the time of my break-up, I had played their deep, painful, soulful music on constant rotation. The irony of the ticket offer, and the fact that they were coming to town, was not lost on me. I was becoming aware of the synchronicities the Universe was gifting me.

A couple of blocks later I arrived at the gallery in the Armoury District. As I entered through the front door I was greeted by Bob, the father of the artist whose work I had come to see. Bob gave me a tour of the studio and described the process his son, Sam, used to make the prints. Sam's specialty was paintings of the Coast Mountains in British Columbia. The studio walls were lined with pieces showcasing the natural beauty of this corner of the world. Towards the end of the tour I saw the piece I had come for. It was even better in person.

The Road to Whistler showed a section of the highway that ran between Vancouver and Whistler, along Howe Sound. In the painting, the highway hugged the mountain-side cliffs, as distant mountains, shrouded in dense clouds, loomed large in the background. It was the lighting of the clouds that drew me in. Foreboding, curling, menacing clouds rolled down the faces of the mountains, revealing a powerful darkness. The darkness in the painting was a direct reflection of my world at that time. While the agony had been intense, the break-throughs, realizations and new awareness were, at times, exhilarating. The hurt was so heavy, that I'd wished it on no one. At the same time, I was conflicted because for brief moments I seemed to be enjoying the clarity that the pain was revealing. I wondered if that was possible. In the centre of the painting, a faint but hopeful light shone through on to a peaceful white cloud, hovering just above the water. A brief glimpse of hope, that the dark storm would soon pass. I loved it. Before leaving the studio, I paid Bob for a framed print and delivery to my condo.

Since I was ahead of schedule and there was a break in the relent-less November rains, I decided to skip the bus and instead make the thirty-minute walk across Burrard Bridge into downtown to meet a friend for lunch. Once I arrived, Jake, a friend since our engineering days, was late as usual. Our long-standing joke, about how he operat-ed on "Jake-time", no longer seemed to bother me. Instead, I took the extra quiet minutes to further practice being present, as I focused on the rich woods and leathers that furnished the restaurant. Jake arrived a few minutes later and we settled into the high-backed chairs at our table and ordered a round of beers.

I filled Jake in, as this was the first time we'd spoken since my sep-aration. He was shocked. Like me, he couldn't understand how things had ended so quickly. "Last time I saw you guys together, a few months ago, everything seemed fine," he said.

My tears came fast and easy. I had no explanation. I started to ponder if I would ever get through another meal without crying. After my tears stopped, Jake shared details about a past breakup of his own, that I had never heard before. Hearing about his struggles, as well as everything he learned and how he grew, brought me some relief about what was going on in my head. This was confirmed for me again when I saw the counselor later that afternoon.

"Wow, can I just say that I am impressed with your progress so far," said the counselor halfway through our session.

I had spent the first part of our time together describing the separation and the pain I was feeling, but also the realizations and clarity I was finding. I described how I was no longer feeling any anger, but instead a sense of relief with each breakthrough about how things had gone wrong. I described how overwhelming it was to have so many painful realizations bombard my mind on a daily basis. "You're not losing your mind, but perhaps, you are finding it," he said.

"But what about the mix-up with the kick-boxing class? That really scares me."

"Just focus on doing a better job with food and sleep. It will get better. However, you are bad at breathing."

"Uh, say what?" I thought I was totally rocking the whole breathing thing.

"Your breathing is shallow, too much in your upper chest. You need to learn how to take fuller, deeper breaths, using your stomach."

I didn't say anything, but I wondered if this could explain the pain in my chest that had been brewing over the past six months. I had ignored the tightness at first, but over the previous months it had grown into sharp pains at different moments throughout the day. I was perplexed and nervous as to what may be causing the discomfort. I had seen different doctors and undergone tests—an ECG and an X-ray— but had not received any meaningful results. I was waiting to book my next appointment—a CT scan—that would hopefully provide some answers.

I left the appointment satisfied that my new glimpses of higher consciousness were not coming at a detriment to my health. While that was reassuring, what I didn't get was a better understanding about what changes were occurring in my mind. What were all these new thoughts I was having? How had I accessed them? How could I go deeper? Who could help me understand more? I asked myself as I started my walk back home.

Later that night back at the condo, deep into a bottle of red wine, I started to write. Even though a few days had passed, my mind was still spinning about the night at Barney's earlier in the week. I had to record the events of the evening. I wrote about how I exited the kick-boxing studio, how I chose right over left, the new friends I connected with, the new world that opened before my eyes. Lying on my living room floor in front of the gas fireplace, I wrote in my journal for over an hour as the emotion poured out. The experience of that night was so powerful. Now having it recorded in words, I felt pulled to share it with someone. I wasn't sure if I was seeking validation that it was in fact a profound evening, or perhaps I was just searching for connection after the separation. Whatever it was, I wanted to share it, but with whom? Who could I trust with my thoughts? Who thought on a similar plane? Who could help me better understand what was going on? The answer was obvious, and a little risky, which added to the excitement. Stacey, the local radio host. I would share my first ever piece of writing with her, the one who posted about seeing and feeling the pain from others "crying in the streets". The one who also shared daily raw and vulnerable posts about her personal struggles with relationships, mental health, and life in general. She would understand these levels of emotion I was feeling, but could I trust her? There was only one way to find out.

"Hey, I wrote something. Can I trust you with it?" I messaged her over social media.

"Of course," she replied.

She shared her email address and I finished typing out what I had written by hand. I hit 'send' on the email just before I fell asleep for the night. I was sending my most personal thoughts and feelings to a total stranger. At the same time, I was learning to trust more openly.

"I know Azalea," read the reply from Stacey the next morning, referring to the woman with the sick dog I had met on that fateful night. How could that be? What greater power was connecting us? First with the proximity of the "crying in the streets" event and now this? I messaged my good friend Max, who also followed Stacey online, to share the latest. "Wizardly," he replied. I fully agreed.

After getting up and making an espresso, I channeled this burst of energy into more writing. I settled in on the living room floor while a classic West Coast storm raged wind and rain against the windows and skylight overhead. It was perfect weather for writing. Opening my journal, I started to write about what drew me to live on the West Coast: the energy. An entire ocean of energy focused and released on the shores, mountains, and inlets. An ocean of wind, rain, waves, and currents. A living ocean of creatures, massive to micro, all full of spirit. An ocean of energy. I was surprised to see what I had written. This was not the me I knew. Where did this clarity to articulate feelings come from? Feelings that must have always been inside, but only ever came out as a grunt. For as long as I could remember, my Mom had been telling me to 'use my words'. Perhaps I was finally starting to listen to her.

Without giving it too much thought, I posted my thoughts on social media for my small circle of friends and family to see if they shared my vibe. Before long I had my answer: they did. In sharing this new type of content, I was learning how to be vulnerable, posting something different than my usual photos of nature or sports. As the feedback started to trickle in, it felt good to have my unique thoughts resonate with others. I also imagined that it made my followers pause, if just for a moment, to consider why they lived where they did. Or if they also lived on the West Coast, could they feel a similar energy?

My retrospection was interrupted by my growling stomach telling me I needed food. As the only contents of my fridge were beer and wine, I got dressed and made my way a half block down West 7th to Wicked Café for a late breakfast. Once inside, I made my first real connection of the day with a younger woman wearing a University of Victoria sweatshirt, my alma mater. "Great school, I did my first engineering degree there," I said.

"Yeah, it's great! I've been loving it," she said, before introducing herself as Mary, while peering over my shoulder at a golden retriever tied up outside of the café.

"That's my dog, Murphy. He's a sweetie," Mary said, as we both looked out the window.

Our conversation was interrupted as we both became aware of the woman in front of us in line. The woman was unleashing her life's frustrations on the innocent barista behind the counter. When she was finished, she collected her drink and stormed out of the café.

"Wow, she had some bad energy," I said to Mary, who nodded in agreement.

I ordered an espresso and a sandwich, then went outside to meet Murphy, and find a seat on the patio. Mary came out soon after, untied Murphy and said goodbye as they started off down the street.

As my meal arrived, I took notice of a middle-aged man to my left wearing a dark ball cap. He sat peacefully, deep in thought, staring out across the street at nothing in particular. Mirroring his demeanor,

I soon found myself lost in thought. My mind became blocked as I searched for a word that I could not find. Sensing that the man beside me may be able to help, I took a chance and asked him, "What is that word when you care more about yourself than others?"

"Hmm, let me think," he replied, becoming just as intrigued to find the elusive word. "By the way, I'm Dave," he added, after a brief silence.

"I'm Mike. It's a pleasure to meet you," I said.

It didn't take long before my new friend and I were connecting on a deeper level. Soon we forgot about our search for the baffling word and started bantering back and forth about other topics. I was amazed how quickly the connection was formed and how he could sense that I was working through something. I shared a bit about my breakup and how I was processing a lot of new thoughts and emotions. Dave then opened to me about his divorce from his wife of thirteen years. It had been a few years since his breakup, but I could feel that pain was still present. We shared a few deep breaths, bonded over broken hearts.

The conversation felt so good, so much better than small-talk, or complaining about the weather. For me, this was a new world of compassion and connecting with strangers. A new world that was unfolding at the same coffee shop I had been going to for years. A new world accessed simply by seeing others, listening to their stories, and being fully present. Before leaving, Dave shared with me about the importance of setting good boundaries. Sensing that I was just at the beginning of my journey into self-awareness, he shared how he had firm boundaries surrounding what he shared with certain people. This was important for me to hear. While it had been feeling so good to share what I had been going through, Dave's point was that there were certain limits to what I needed to share. In addition, I would have to learn who to share with and at what level, as some friends and family wouldn't be used to, or ready to hear about my bleeding heart. I would also have to think about how much I would share with my wife.

The depths of these new connections came so naturally but were also exhausting. After saying goodbye to Dave, I made the short walk back to the condo. After finishing a journal entry about the latest connection, I made my way to the chaise for a much-needed power nap, before a planned dinner with my wife.

Since the breakup, my wife and I had been trying to give each other space, while also trying to understand how this could have happened. It had been a little over a week since she had walked out on our twelve-year relationship. We had only been communicating by text during that time, and that wasn't working. She had been trying to explain herself and I had been reading her messages in disbelief. We agreed that meeting in person would be best. We decided to meet at a neutral location, a sports bar on Main Street. I arrived to find her sitting at a booth in the back corner of the bar. She'd been crying. We both had.

"This won't work, this space," I said, overwhelmed by the noise and the distraction of a hockey game on the TV, not to mention the nearby table of drunks. I didn't want any distractions; I was there to focus on this conversation and nothing else. We looked around for a quieter seat but couldn't see any better options. I closed my eyes and took a few deeps breaths, before calming down. We decided to stay put and make it work.

"My mind is blown, you are so different," she said, with a look of shock. She was used to the old Mike, the Mike that would sleepily stare at the hockey game to avoid all conversation. Instead, I kept all my attention on her. To see her tears, to feel her pain. I was there to understand why she left, something she herself was still coming to terms with. By being fully present and not reacting in anger, I created a safe space for her to speak her mind. As much as it hurt to hear her words, they needed to be spoken. At the same time, I wondered if I was just suppressing my pain, my anger. Was I trying to prove to her that I could be the partner that she wanted? Someone who could listen and not react in anger? Was I subconsciously tormenting her by showing the transformed me, that she was missing out on? Sitting in the booth, I realized that one of the reasons we never really talked was because I never really listened. Or if I disagreed with her, I would get defensive and react in anger. Two ways to immediately shut down any connection.

With my conversation with Dave in the back of my mind, I respected my boundaries when she began to press about what I had been up to. As good as it felt to connect on a real level, I had to remember that she had just thrown my whole world upside-down. Where I would once not hesitate to share my day with her, I drew a line in the sand and shared nothing about my tearful dinners with friends, connecting with strangers at bars and cafés, or about my new art. This would be our new relationship going forward. As much as it may have hurt her not to know what I had been up to, it hurt me even more not to be able to share. But I had to be firm and establish a new boundary. There were no winners in this situation. It was only later when we realized how enriched we both were by this whole ordeal.

She shared a little about what she had been up to. She explained the feelings and emotions that she had been working through, including the realization about how she craved deeper connection, both from a partner and others in her world. I had already heard most of this by text, but I listened and helped where I could. What she couldn't give was a clear answer about why she was choosing to pursue a different life.

We discussed what she was learning about herself and the books she was reading to go deeper into her self-exploration. She shared an excerpt from one of the books on the six traits that all humans need to be happy: certainty, uncertainty/variety, significance, love/connections, growth, and contribution. We were trying to help each other handle the breakup, which was equally comforting and confusing, especially considering how new this all was. It was almost as though we were more focused on our individual journeys of self-discovery than we were on trying to save the relationship. As she spoke, I wondered if this reflected our twelve years together, both focused more on ourselves than the relationship.

After dinner we agreed that continuing to live separately was best for the immediate future. I walked her to her car where we shared a long hug before I turned and walked away. On my walk home she sent me a text: "I'm excited for you and your awakening. You deserve connection too. I didn't realize you were missing it as well." It was ironic, the connection that I didn't even realize I was missing, the same connection that was missing in our relationship, I was learning how to access only after it was too late.

———————

The next morning, I met Jake for a trail run in the forested park near the university. The dense canvas of trees and the soft gravel trails were a runner's delight. During the run I mentioned my conversation with Dave and the mysterious word we could not find.

"Self-serving," said Jake without hesitation.

"That's it!" I yelled. "Man, you're sharp."

Self-serving. That's how I had been living until that moment with Dave. In that moment I realized that my thoughts and actions could no longer be purely for my benefit. I could no longer live in a self-serving manner. I could not stop connecting with others and wanting to help them. As good as it felt to have this clarity, it also hurt like hell to realize this was how I had been operating all those years.

Deep into the wine later that night at the condo, I lay on the living room floor writing in my journal, reflecting on the past couple of weeks. "A True Awakening," I wrote as music filled the candle-lit condo with heavy base and energetic rhythms. I was listening to a playlist from my friends in Toronto. I'd been using all my friends to get me through this trail of pain. The hurt had continued to surface at different times throughout my days. At times, my mind would wander to the past and good memories my wife and I had shared. Grief would hit me like a ton of bricks.

Several times at work over the past couple of weeks I'd escaped to hide in the bathroom as the waves of pain rolled through me. At other times, my mind would drift to the uncertainty of the future and the upcoming holidays, which would be spent alone. Often, I was around other people when these thoughts came up. I had been working on stopping the train of thoughts, by focusing on taking deep, cleansing breaths. It was working to an extent, but I had a long way to go.

Christmas was around the corner, so I had hung Christmas lights around the living room window to add some cheer. Through the window, I could see the lights on the condo tower construction cranes across False Creek. Dark clouds moved slowly over the city. A city that was brimming with energy before the holiday season. The view and the energy, both inside and outside the condo, was heavy.

The intensity of the early days following the separation was beginning to wane. But as the reality of the situation became more real, it was almost as though my newfound awareness, the processing and trying to understand my thoughts, was my new companion. Was this new awareness of any use, or was it just distracting me from the pain and the hurt? I had so many thoughts pulsing through my mind. I was tired, exhausted, drained, scared, and alone, but in that moment, lying on the living room floor, I was not lonely.

My mind wandered for a moment to the limitless possibilities of this new world I found myself in. Art, music, travel—I now had the freedom to pursue whatever I wanted. A freedom that I never wanted, but that now appeared to be mine. The moment of excitement was short lived, as a crush of sorrow landed in my soul. How did all this happen? It was only a few months ago that we were talking about having a baby and buying a bigger home. How could this have unravelled so quickly? I felt like I had been cheated out of a perfect future.

As the tears subsided, I wrote in my journal about what had been unlocked: I could feel song lyrics, I could write and express my feelings, I could help people open up about their struggles, I could cry freely in restaurants and on the streets, I was becoming more aware of my thoughts, I was gaining clarity—clarity that had been blocked by life's distractions, and my own self-serving ego. The clarity felt good. I was excited with the awakening, but also terrified when I did feel alone. If this unwanted freedom was here to stay, it was my opportunity to live fully and completely.

I was experiencing glimpses of hope and optimism, mixed with the sadness. For brief moments I could imagine new possibilities before my current reality settled back in. I had been spending a lot of time lying on the living room floor, staring up at the skylight, as the November rains poured down their pain. I knew I didn't want to stay there, on the floor. I was no good to others in a crumbled heap of hurt. I was of no use if I let this situation destroy my mind. I knew I had to tap into my new thoughts, to lift myself off the ground. If something external had happened, to put me in this state, why couldn't I generate something internally to lift myself out? I had to be stronger than my pain.

So many friends and family had sent their love during those tough times, it had made all the difference. I had to be stronger, for them. I had to tap into the love that they sent, to pick myself up. I was grateful to have them in my life. There was never any doubt that they were there for me. The unconditional support from family and friends was something I couldn't even imagine not having. Something that, I would eventually learn, others were not as fortunate to have.

I always knew there was more to life. I had felt it in my bones. I wanted it, but never imagined I needed trauma to unleash it. I had entered a new life of living at emotional extremes. I would never go back to vanilla and comfortable.

Lying on the living room carpet, staring up at the sky, I vowed to learn and grow from this destructive experience, to piece myself back together to emerge as the best version of me. I knew that to create this new version of me I had to leave my self-serving ways behind and find a way to serve others. What I didn't know at the time, was how best to do that.

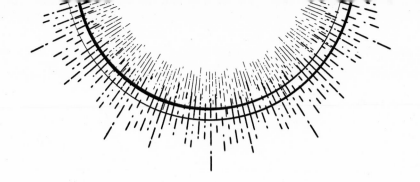

CHAPTER 3

FROM WITHIN

*The real voyage of discovery consists not in seeking
new landscapes, but in having new eyes.*

MARCEL PROUST

The high of my November revelations was replaced with the low of my sad new reality. The sentiment came to the surface, as the first heavy chord played at The National concert. The intimate view from row eight at the small theatre only added depth to the show. The opening song sent tears down my face. I was not alone with this raw feeling, on the first weekend in December. To my left, was a young man who was also at the concert on his own. To my right were two young women, gazing straight ahead as tears rolled down their faces. The dark music evoked further pain within me, but I sensed it needed to be felt before I could move on.

The National had become a quick favourite since being introduced to me. The lyrics from the baritone voice of the lead singer had been talking to me over the past month. One song, called "About Today", described how his marriage almost slipped away. The lyrics spoke of a distance that had formed between him and his wife. At first, he didn't ask about the void, but this changed towards the end of the song, when he confronted her one night before bed.

As the song played, I wondered, was this where I went wrong in my relationship? Could I have been more aware about the distance that was so obviously growing? Was there something I could have said before it was too late? If I had taken a stand against the distance that was growing would it have made a difference? I cried all the way through the song as I replayed the last few months in my mind.

Toward the end of the show my phone vibrated with an incoming text from a friend, Jeremy: "Hey buddy, how are you doing? Just checking in."

"I'm a proper mess. I'm at a concert right now. I'll give you a call after the show," I replied.

After the band finished their set, I exited the theatre into a light rain. I found a concrete barricade to lean against and dialed Jeremy's number. Jeremy was in Thailand at the time, recharging after a challenging year of his own. I had no idea what time it was over there and didn't expect him to answer a call from Canada. He answered after the second ring. I burst into a fresh round of tears at the sound of his voice. I had such amazing friends.

As the tears rolled out, Jeremy encouraged me to keep feeling the waves of emotions and let the pain run its course. He'd been there before, after his brother took his own life. After that happened, part of

Jeremy's healing was to channel his pain into setting up a trust fund for people with mental health-related challenges. Jeremy's courage to take on this initiative, while still processing his own grief, was admirable.

I used my sleeve to wipe the tears from my face as we ended our call. I pushed off the concrete barrier I was leaning against and started to walk. The crowd that was still exiting the concert was full of energy, making their way to the nearby bars for more drinking, singing, and dancing. Not me; I put my hood up, my headphones on, and started the long walk across downtown towards the condo.

The next morning, I met with Ash for coffee on Main Street. As soon as I saw her inside the café, I knew that something was up. She was in love. After we got our coffees, she shared all about her new man. As she spoke as I sipped my espresso with shaking hands—a result of lack of sleep and too much to drink during the concert the night before. Ash was beaming. I was beyond happy for her. In years past, I would have only focused on myself and my shit situation, while faking joy for her. Not anymore. I genuinely shared her energy, as she described the meaningful connection she had found, after years of struggling to find the magic. She gave me hope that my wounded heart would love again.

After coffee I drove out to the airport to pick up my father. Dad was flying in for the weekend from Ontario, for the Toronto Maple Leafs vs. Vancouver Canucks hockey game. My sister and her family were also coming over from Vancouver Island for the game. I knew the game was merely a cover; they were really coming to town to make sure I was okay. I appreciated their concern but was nervous about seeing them for the first time since the separation.

Dad's flight was on time and he was waiting outside the terminal by the time I arrived. I was anxious to see him, and I must have looked like a train wreck. I parked and got out of the truck to exchange a brief

hug. Dad hadn't eaten so we got into the truck and started the drive
back towards downtown and his favourite restaurant on Granville Island. A creature of habit, Dad was never too interested in exploring
new spots. (Not that I was exactly up to date with Vancouver's latest
culinary trends.)

Arriving at the restaurant, I remembered why we both loved it:
the view from the rooftop patio of the passing boats in False Creek was
soothing and magical. "It sure doesn't look like this in frozen Ontario
right now," he said, as we took our seats outside under the heat lamps.

The weather, we always talked about the weather. I knew the
weather; I was sitting in it. I'd always wanted to go deeper with Dad,
with all my family members. We were all capable of deeper conversations, we all had them with other people. But for some reason we always
remained at the surface with each other. Maybe now that I was learning
to tap into deeper connections, we would finally be able to have those
meaningful conversations and I could ask the questions that had remained untouched. Questions like, what really happened between you
and Mom when you divorced? Do you have any regrets? Why are you
still carrying the grief? As much as I wanted to dive straight into this
real talk, it still seemed a distance away.

"Have you thought about getting your own lawyer?" Dad asked,
after our food arrived.

"Well, I've thought about it, but that's as far as I've gone, Dad," I
replied, grateful to move on from the weather talk.

With a successful career as a lawyer and now a judge, I took full
advantage of his free advice. "Do you know any lawyers out here?" I
asked.

As Dad thought on my request, I became aware that we had drifted into a conversation of more substance. It was ironic that the connec-

tion between his legal expertise and my separation may be the bridge to lift our relationship to a new level. Perhaps some good would come out of all of this.

After we finished lunch, Dad and I made our way downtown to meet my sister and her family at their hotel. Once her kids were set up with the babysitter, my sister Jenn, her husband Scott, along with Dad and myself, left the hotel and started the short walk to the arena for the start of the hockey game.

As we took our seats, I became aware that the afternoon start-time had not deterred many of the fans from arriving several beers deep. Before the game even started, we were serenaded by the drunk fans in the row behind us. At the same time, I hadn't even been able to talk to my sister or Scott about the separation. The timing wasn't right at the hotel with the kids around, and it certainly wasn't the right time at the hockey game.

With each minute that ticked by I could feel my chest grow tighter. Tension was growing within me about not being able to address the elephant in the room, or in our case, the arena. While we didn't excel at having the hard conversations, I still wondered why they hadn't yet asked me if I was okay. Before the puck was even dropped, I knew the game was going to be a struggle for me to get through.

The first two periods were unmemorable. The second period ended with the Canucks up by two goals. I spent most of the game staring into the rafters overhead, wondering what I was doing there. I couldn't bring myself to care about a puck going into a net, given that I was crumbling on the inside. I repeatedly took deep breaths, supressing my emotions. A different scenario than the dark concert hall the night before, I didn't want to be the only one in the arena bawling my eyes out.

I used to love going to hockey games; I used to love being one of the drunks that cared about the score. For years I had spent hours watching the Leafs. I would plan entire weekends around their Saturday night games. But now, something had changed. While I valued time with my family, in that moment, I would have given anything to get out of that rink.

Things got interesting towards the end of the third period when the Leafs scored to make it a one goal game. As the Leafs continued to press, I briefly forgot about my sorrow and became interested in the game. With the clock ticking down over the final minutes, the Leafs gave a final push to try and tie the score. We were all on our feet in the final minute with a face-off in the Canucks' end. The Leafs won the draw, then had two shots blocked in the final ten seconds. The final buzzer sounded; the Canucks had won the game. The Leaf fans around us swore in anger at the loss. While I had enjoyed the brief escape from my thoughts, I had bigger things to get upset about.

After the game we made our way back to the hotel restaurant for dinner. I sat beside my two nieces, as they worked on their colouring. They didn't ask why Rebecca, my wife, wasn't with me. Which was good because I didn't have a good answer. Halfway through dinner my phone vibrated, with a text from another friend, Brooke: "when are you coming home?"

Brooke was a friend since elementary school back in Kingston, where we all grew up. She'd obviously heard about the breakup, but had kept her distance, until now.

"I'm not," I replied.

I had thought about going home to Kingston over the holidays, like I usually did, but had decided I just couldn't handle seeing all my friends, plus the rest of my family. Another factor was the two ski trips I already had booked around that time. The cost of a trip to Kingston did not make sense for such a short stay. Instead my plan was to suffer through the holidays alone in Vancouver.

"Wrong answer, buddy," Brooke replied. Always one to speak her mind, she wasn't going to accept my answer. "I'm going to keep asking you, bucko," Brooke promised.

Jenn's kids started to get tired, so we finished dinner and paid the bill. It was great to have the kids there, but it also meant the rest of us couldn't talk about the real reason we had gotten together. After we said our goodbyes, I made my way outside into the expected rain. I was in no rush to get home to my empty condo. Just like the night before, I decided to skip the bus and make the forty-five-minute walk across downtown towards home.

After twenty minutes I made my way onto the Granville Bridge and felt the first blast of wind whipping the rain into my face. The rinsing was refreshing, and for a moment brought my attention away from my misery. My mind turned to the communication blocks I had with my family. Having recognized that my inability to adequately communicate had contributed to the end of my marriage, I had to find a way to break through this barrier with my family. Why was it that I still couldn't connect with them, like I did with others? Was I forever stuck in my old self when in their presence? Would we ever be able to speak the unspoken words that lay below the surface?

As I made my way off the bridge onto Hemlock Street, several limousines streamed in the opposite direction back towards downtown. It was the first weekend of December, so I assumed the cars were full of partiers kicking off the holiday season. That could be me I thought, as I remembered that my holiday office party was well underway, without me. I had a legitimate excuse to skip the event, as my family was in town. In years past, I would often strategically plan a ski trip, so I could avoid the awkward event. Along with office birthday parties, the annual holiday party was something I never looked forward to. I wondered if I was the only one who felt this way. Again, I never felt like I could truly connect with my engineering colleagues, plus, we didn't have many things in common. My friends outside of work had always remarked that I didn't look like an engineer. Maybe they were right. Either way, I was in no mood to celebrate, as I trudged the final few blocks back to the dark, empty condo.

Sunday morning arrived with the promise of a new day and a rare December bright sunrise. Opening my eyes, I saw the long-forgotten sunlight stream between my bedroom curtains. I sprung out of bed and made my way to the kitchen to bring the espresso machine to life. After grinding the beans, I made myself a fresh double shot. I walked with my mug through the small dining and living areas, and onto the outdoor deck. Looking east down False Creek, I saw the growing light bring the distant mountains to life. Despite the darkness that had entered the condo in the past few months, mornings like this reminded me how fortunate I was to live where I did.

My thoughts turned to my wife, who had been bouncing between friends' couches and her parents' home just outside of Vancouver. Over the previous weeks she had texted saying that she was displaced, with nowhere to feel grounded. Despite the pain she had caused me, it still hurt to know that she was also suffering.

She had told me her latest plan was to move back to her hometown, Kamloops, for the spring. She had realized that the city wasn't for her, that she was more comfortable in smaller towns. On the other hand, since our separation, I began to realize that I craved the energy of the city. We had long discussed where our future would be, but neither of us had been clear on what we wanted. Instead, we spent years in endless debate of city versus country, only to end up with neither. The reality was, I would have moved anywhere for her.

With my espresso in hand, I came back inside. I took a seat in front of the fireplace on a blue foam roller—a tool I used for managing sore muscles while training for an Ironman race a year earlier. I had enjoyed the process of training, as I learned how far I could push my body. But there was no life-altering euphoria when I crossed the finish line at the end of the race; I only remembered feeling empty. Sitting on the foam roller I shook my head at the new realization: the months of training were partially an escape to avoid other parts of my life that were falling apart. My wife always complained that I had no energy left for her, after hours of training. As agonizing as it was to arrive at this clarity about our past, it also helped add further explanation to what small pieces had contributed to our ultimate downfall.

Back in the present moment, I opened a meditation application on my phone that I had been testing for a couple of weeks. I had previously tried meditation, only to quit after not achieving instant enlightenment. Recognizing that I could benefit from better managing the swirling thoughts in my mind, I had now found better consistency with this new app.

I loaded a meditation and closed my eyes sitting cross-legged on the foam roller. The voice on the meditation guided me to visualize myself as a tall mountain, standing strong, dignified, and firmly rooted to the earth. In my mind's eye, I saw myself as a mountain, like the one in Sam's painting that hung on my wall. A lush, green west coast mountain, with streams running through the valleys, emptying into the ocean below. Above the treeline, tall, barren, rocky peaks reached for the sky above. As I looked down from the peak of the mountain, I watched as the leaves on the trees changed with the passing seasons. I saw the streams freeze over with winter ice and snow. From my vantage at the summit, I saw the winter storms rage on the highest peaks and send avalanches into the valleys below. In the spring, the snow melted and once again filled the streams with rushing water. Summer arrived and the streams dried up, with the heat from the sun. Through the changing seasons, the storms, and the droughts, I sat still as the mountain. Strong, calm, firmly rooted to the earth, connected to Mother Nature by my breath. I remained peaceful on the inside, even as fury raged on my surface.

After twenty minutes, the meditation ended with the sound of a soft chiming bell. I loved this moment. Only once I was ready, I would slowly open my eyes and look out the living room window. In those first moments I would see the condo towers and the mountains in the distance with a new degree of clarity. I felt completely calm and at peace.

Energized by the morning and the December sun, I again chose to skip the bus—which I normally took during the wet months—in favour of another walk across the bridge. I was headed downtown to meet the family and watch the Santa Claus Parade. Along the way I paused several times to take pictures with my phone, as the sun dried out the water-logged city. By the time I reached my family, they had already seen enough of the parade. Leaving the parade and the crowds behind, we regrouped back at their hotel for a swim. The swim was brief, as they had to make their way home to Victoria, on Vancouver Island. Before they left, Jenn and I made plans to go for dinner, without the kids, when I was in Victoria later in the week. A dinner without the kids would allow us to talk about what was on everybody's mind—my separation.

Dad wasn't leaving until the next day, so after Jenn and her family left, we headed to the hotel restaurant for lunch. We took two seats at the bar and each ordered a beer. As our drinks arrived, he turned towards me and softly asked, "So, how are you really doing?"

That's all it took for the tears to pour out, in the middle of the day, in a brightly lit restaurant full of strangers. I could cry anywhere these days. I didn't even try to hold it back. My body trembled, exhausted with the emotions from the weekend. I leaned forward to rest my head on my arms, which were folded on the bar. "This fucking sucks," I replied.

"It sure does," he answered, as he reached over to rub my back.

While we sometimes struggled to find the words to convey what we were feeling, there was never a lack of love between my father and me.

After lunch, Dad and I walked twenty minutes across town, for a matinee performance at Cirque du Soleil. Our first stop inside the circus tent was at the bar, where we each ordered a glass of wine. The first glass went down easily, so I convinced myself that a second glass would only enhance the show. Two sips into the second glass, I instantly regretted this plan. The volume of alcohol from the weekend—starting with the concert Friday, the hockey game and dinner Saturday, followed by lunch and the circus on Sunday—was starting to accumulate in a headache above my left eye. I had been drinking more than usual. I figured I had a good enough excuse. Plus, I was worried that my realizations would stop if I wasn't consistently buzzed. Either way, it was becoming too much.

The show was decent and for once I made an effort to follow the story line. At each Cirque show that I had previously seen, I had always been impressed with the fitness of the performers. I could do this, I could be happy doing this, I thought during the show. For the first time in my life, I could see myself doing something other than engineering.

After the show, Dad and I shared a taxi back to his hotel, where we said our goodbyes. He was leaving early the next morning, so I would not see him again. It was a short visit, but I was grateful he came out to check on me, and I knew his mind was put somewhat at ease seeing me in person. I continued in the taxi for my final crossing of the Granville Bridge that weekend. "A concert, hockey game, dinner and the circus; it's been a full couple of days," I explained to the taxi driver, after he asked about my weekend.

"Wow, lucky guy," he said.

"Indeed, I am. They were perfect distractions," I replied, as our eyes met in the rear-view mirror. I could sense he knew there was more to the story. We finished chatting and the taxi driver stopped in front of the condo. I paid for the ride and opened the door to get out. Before I got out, the driver turned to me and said, "I like you, man. I like your energy. I like your smile." This surprised me. What was this magical world unfolding around me? As I made my way up the stairs to the condo, I reflected on the surprising connection in the taxi, the love from my family, and the weekend's events. All of it gave me a little hope, that I was going to get through this.

———

A couple of days later at work, my boss called me into her office. Once inside, she surprised me with an annual bonus that was four times my usual amount. Ever since I had started speaking my mind and being more myself, my impact around the office had been noticeable. It wasn't just my clients that were attracted to my new energy, but my co-workers fed off it as well. "You have evolved," said my boss, during our short meeting. If only she knew the whole story. I bit my tongue and decided to stick with my plan of waiting until the new year to share the details of my separation. It had almost been a month since the split, and I had managed to keep it hidden from everyone at work.

Before leaving her office, I gave my boss an update on my projects. I shared with her that my main project was scheduled to start construction, in Victoria, early in the new year. It was my turn to surprise her when I mentioned that I planned to nominate myself as the engineer on-site for the three-month project. I could sense that she was curious about me wanting to be away from home for so long, but she did not question it. It was my choice to take the role, and I knew a change of scenery was exactly what I needed. It would be an escape from my familiar life in Vancouver. All I needed to do was put my head down and get through the last couple weeks of the year. I was hoping that a new start in Victoria would help me leave some of the pain behind in Vancouver.

Back in my own office, I reflected on the extra money that was coming my way. It was going to be nice, but it wouldn't heal my wounds. In addition to stepping more into an authentic leadership role, I also knew the extra recognition was related to getting through a challenging situation earlier in the year. When another one of my projects was nearing completion, I started to get in over my head. As the target completion date for the project approached, the contractor started to run into several challenges. Instead of giving the required extra hours to work through the problem, I became distant, and uninterested. The client was not impressed.

After a team meeting, my client pulled me into a private boardroom, for a one-on-one grilling about my lack of commitment to the project. It shook me to my core. But he was right, and it was exactly what I needed to start that first crack in my corporate shell. I refocused after our chat and saw the project through to a successful completion.

I had survived and was being rewarded for my perseverance. Sitting at my desk I wondered what to do with the extra money. With the first three months of the new year committed to the project in Victoria, maybe I could treat myself to a trip in the spring? The thought excited me, before dejection set in, with the realization that I would be traveling alone.

A couple of days after the meeting with my boss, I was back in the counselor's office for our follow-up appointment. Part way through the meeting we were still struggling to pin-point exactly how he could serve me. "So, what exactly can I help you with?" he asked. By the tone of his voice I could tell he was starting to get impatient with me.

"I just want to fully get to know the real me," I explained.

"That is the best answer I have ever got from that question," he replied.

It was true, the problem was, I didn't know how to keep going deeper, to uncover the true me. Ever since the separation I had been figuring things out on my own. The meditation was starting to help me become more aware of my thoughts. It was also helping to calm my racing mind. I was meditating most mornings for up to twenty minutes at a time. I was getting a better hold on my thoughts, but once I had a grip on them, I didn't know what to do with them. On top of that, I was struggling to comprehend how I could observe my thoughts as if they were separate from me. I had never given it much consideration; I had always assumed that my mind, my brain, my thoughts, all that mess, were connected and formed who I was. Now it was as though I was the one observing the thoughts, as if they were separate from me. I was confused. I needed help to understand.

Unfortunately, the counselor didn't have too much more to offer towards progressing my transforming mind. As our session came to an end he lit up with excitement and said, "Have you read *The Untethered Soul*[1]? You have to check it out."

"I've never heard of it. What's it about?" I asked.

"It's about the relationship between your thoughts and who you really are. It helps you understand how your habitual thoughts and emotions can limit your consciousness. I think it will help you on your journey."

"Sounds intriguing. I'll for sure pick up a copy," I said, getting up out of my chair and making my way towards the office door. We agreed that I probably wouldn't benefit from another session with him. While he hadn't been able to answer all the questions in my head, he had provided reassurance that I was on the right path.

As a test run for my longer stay in the new year, I headed over to Victoria at the end of the second week in December. I would be relieving a co-worker from a construction project that was already underway. For three days I would be on a barge in Victoria's Inner Harbour, monitoring dredging of contaminated materials from the ocean floor. After taking the ferry over from the mainland, I drove into town with great expectations for a sample of what my new surroundings would

---

1 Singer, Michael A. *The Untethered Soul: The Journey Beyond Yourself.* Oakland, CA: New Harbinger Publications, 2007.

offer. My new beginnings started by checking into the classy Magnolia Hotel. The heritage building was known for its classic architecture, high ceilings and elegant furniture. It was exactly the change of style I was craving.

Soon after checking in, I made the short walk to Trounce Alley to meet Jenn and Scott for dinner. With their kids at home with a babysitter, we would finally be able to talk. All the tables were taken, so we took the last remaining seats at the bar. The restaurant was pulsing with hurried servers and lively music. "So, what the heck happened?" Jenn asked, getting right into it.

"Well," I began, "I guess she wanted to live a different life."

"But we just saw you guys in Tofino in October."

"Ya, and did you notice how distant she was? She had already checked out, her mind was made up."

"So, how are you?"

"Most days are real shit. But it's getting better. It just happened so fast. Remember that weekend I was in California at the beginning of November? When I came back from that, she was done with it all. It totally sucks."

"That's so hard. I'm so sorry. That totally bites."

"It sure does."

"So, is that it? Is it over between you two?"

"I don't know, I mean, I think so. She's talking about moving to Kamloops, to see how she likes living in a smaller city. So ya, I guess it is," I said, with a heavy sigh.

"What now?" asked Scott.

"Well, I've got two ski trips booked around Christmas, then it looks like I'll be back here, in Victoria, for three months of work," I said.

"That'll be a good change, won't it?" asked Scott.

"Sure will. I'm looking forward to it. It'll be good to see you guys, and your kids," I said.

After dinner was over, Jenn and Scott headed home and I met up with my friend, Justin. I had been nervous about committing to spend time with him. His perpetual funk radiated negative energy. It always drained me. But he was a friend who I cared about; a friend, who I knew had immeasurable value to gift to the world, once he broke out of his funk. With all the changes I had been experiencing, my hope was that I could positively influence him to make some changes in his world.

Justin met me outside the restaurant, where we debated which bar to head to. "Dude, we have to go to the Canoe Club, it always had a good crowd," said Justin.

"That was over a decade ago, man. That was the university crowd, and it probably still is," I argued.

"Ah come on, you'll love it," said Justin.

"Whatever you say, man, you're the one who lives here," I said.

I agreed to go with his choice, and we made the ten-minute walk across downtown. Once we were inside my suspicions were confirmed: the place was full, and it appeared as though the crowd had stayed the same age over the past decade. I felt old and wanted to leave. At the same time, I was in Victoria to get a sample of my new beginnings, which meant putting myself out there and meeting new people.

We took a seat at a round table near the middle of the bar. We both ordered two beers each. To our right, a small group filled the dance floor in front of the cover band. After he finished his beers, Justin headed out to join them. I couldn't bring myself to go with him. It didn't feel right that I had ended up back at a bar that we had frequented during our university days. I was looking for a new start, not a step backwards. Justin didn't share my thoughts. He stayed out on the dance floor, enjoying himself. It was good to see him happy. I stayed behind at the table and continued to order myself drinks, waiting for something magical to happen.

The *magic* happened the next day when I was at work on the contractor's barge, floating in the middle of the harbour. After all the drinking the night before, I had felt off all morning. As the morning wore on, things went from bad to worse. The pain in my head migrated towards my stomach. When I couldn't take it any longer, I snuck off to the downstairs bathroom, where I threw-up most of the booze from the night before. "Fuck this," I muttered to myself, in between dry heaves.

Thankfully, the noise of the machinery drowned out my lack of professionalism. The heaving finally stopped, and I sat slumped on the dirty floor, my face covered in sweat. "This will not do. This is not me. I can do better than this," I said to myself. Sitting in my new low point, I realized that a change of scenery was not going to be my saviour. If I was going to create a new beginning, it would have to come from within.

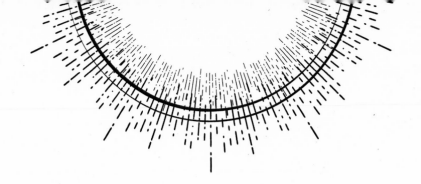

CHAPTER 4

PRESENT MOMENT

If you are depressed you are living in the past.
If you are anxious you are living in the future.
If you are at peace you are living in the present.

LAO TZU

Back in Vancouver a few days later, I made a visit to my hairdresser. I wanted to see Caitie before heading out with friends on a back-country ski trip and into the holiday season. It would be the first time seeing her since the split, so I was nervous about how to fill her in. I was also nervous thinking ahead to the ski trip, and how that was going to go. After my unsuccessful trip to Victoria, I was even getting anxious thinking ahead to the time I was going to spend there in the new year. When I wasn't getting overwhelmed projecting into the future, often my mind would wander to the past, to the marriage, and all the love that had been lost. I was bouncing between a painful past and an unknown future; it was a tough way to exist.

I arrived at my appointment on time and was ushered into Caitie's chair. After she washed my hair, she set to work taming my mane. I filled her in on my news, which she received with both shock and compassion. She had a unique gift to make her clients feel safe and special while in her chair. It didn't take long before we had moved on to joking about the situation. Caitie even tried to lift my spirits at the prospect of a return to dating. "You've got to be an alley cat!" she said, halfway through the appointment. "You've been a house cat for a while now, it's time to be an alley cat!"

"Ha-ha, you're too much," I laughed, at her dating analogy.

I had given some thought to what it was going to be like to date again, and it wasn't a thought I embraced. It all seemed too soon, too overwhelming. It had been over twelve years since I had been on a date. I didn't know much, but I did know that things had changed during that time. On top of that, I was never especially good at dating, it didn't come naturally. Still, the thought of being an *alley cat* sounded intriguing, but it was too soon.

An hour with Caitie was always full of high energy and meaningful conversation. I often felt like a different person when I was in her chair. In her presence, I found it easy to be open, express my feelings, and have real talk. We never spent any time on surface-level conversation. Why did this come so easily with her, but not with my family? Perhaps I'd always had more inside of me, perhaps I could be more like Caitie: a catalyst for meaningful conversation and positive radiant energy. That was the connected world that I wanted so badly. I pondered all of this, as she finished my cut.

The next few days were spent in a whirlwind of packing for a week at a remote private cabin. Since getting into backcountry skiing several years ago, my friends and I had recently taken it to the next level, by renting out helicopter-accessed private cabins. We would be in the backcountry, so there wouldn't be any lifts to access the skis runs. This meant hour-long strenuous climbs up the mountains using climbing skins attached to our skis. It was hard work, but the untracked powder snow made it all worthwhile. The best part about these week-long trips was that we were out of cell phone range, disconnected from the outside world. This disconnection from life's distractions allowed for more connection with nature, and with the others on the trip.

The day arrived to leave for my trip. To break up the eight-hour drive from Vancouver on the coast, to Nelson in the BC Interior, I stopped in Kelowna to spend the night with my good friend, Chris. I arrived at his house just in time for a dinner with him and his wife, Carolyn, and their two girls. Once dinner was over, Chris and I moved to their downstairs living room. Carolyn joined soon after putting the kids to bed.

"So, are you excited to date again?" asked Chris.

"Shit man, that's the second time that's come up this week. I feel it's still way too soon. But I mean, I guess so," I said.

"The making out, that's what you'll enjoy the most!" said Carolyn.

"Ha-ha, if you say so."

"Ah, Mike, you'll be fine. You're a good guy, just let some time pass," said Chris.

"Thanks man, it might take a while,"

"Absolutely. We're going to turn in, you have everything you need?" asked Chris.

"Ya man, I'm all good. I'll see you guys in the morning."

Chris and Carolyn made their way back to the kitchen to finish cleaning up. I was left alone to settle in on the futon Chris had made up for me. As I was putting my head down on the pillow, my phone vibrated with an incoming text message, it was Brooke again. "WHEN ARE YOU COMING HOME FOR CHRISTMAS?" read the text, in capital letters.

"You're a persistent one, AREN'T YOU?" I replied, mirroring her capitals.

"Bite me. Come home. It will be good for you," she texted.

Just as I was coming up with a witty reply, a new text message arrived, this time from Mom: "come home."

Mom was always straight to the point; she didn't waste any time. Did I really want to spend a miserable Christmas alone back in Vancouver, just to save a little bit of money? Screw it, I thought. I sat up from bed, opened my laptop, and booked a flight home to Kingston for Christmas day.

"Okay, Mom, it's booked," I texted to her.

"YAY," she replied.

"I'll be home Christmas Day, you happy?" I messaged Brooke.

"YES! Well done," she replied.

I closed my laptop and put down my phone, before laying my head in an exhausted heap on to the pillow. After this first ski trip, I would be going home for a short Christmas visit. My first Christmas without a partner in over twelve years.

———

After a week of perfect skiing, we flew out of the mountains by helicopter the morning of December 23rd. I had only shared the news of my separation with my two closest friends on the trip. I didn't want to burden the dozen others (most of whom I had just met) with my heartache. Despite not sharing, I was able to build a good connection with these new friends over the week.

As the chopper touched down at the heliport, I exhaled a big sigh of relief after another backcountry ski trip safely completed. Back in cell phone range for the first time in a week, everyone turned on their phones to catch up on messages and to let their loved ones know they were safe. I turned on my phone, scanned through some messages, then let my family know I was safely out of the mountains. But that was it, there was no one else waiting to hear from me. This was the first ski trip that I didn't have a partner to call, to tell how much they were missed. There were no love messages waiting on my phone. Again, I felt empty.

I had also felt this same void during the week of skiing. On the long, hard climbs to the top of our runs, I would search my mind for something positive to focus on. On previous ski trips, I would always think of her, my wife, and our life together. I would think about our future travels plans, or I would think about us starting a family, about growing old together. On this trip, I had to learn to put those thoughts out of my mind; they were just too painful. As soon as I sensed thoughts about her emerging, I would take a deep breath and find something else to focus on. Usually I would focus on the beauty of the nature surrounding me: the mountains, the trees, the peace that was plentiful in the backcountry. It was a good technique, but it wasn't perfect.

Once all the gear was unloaded from the helicopter, we packed our cars, said our goodbyes, and set out for the long drive back to Vancouver. Halfway through the drive, I stopped in Osoyoos for some caffeine. A winery-filled dreamscape in the summer, the town was grey, cold, and desolate during the winter months. The days were short at this time of year and it was already dark by the time I rolled into town.

I was exhausted and considered getting a motel for the night and doing the rest of the drive in the morning. Driving through town I was too tired to decide on where to stay. I resolved to get some food and an extra-large coffee, then keep on driving.

I made a quick pit stop and got back on the road. A few minutes into the drive out of town, the highway took a long, slow climb up Richter Pass—it was the same mountain Mom had ridden on her bike when she used to do the local Ironman race. She had been my inspiration to do an Ironman. Even though she was in her sixties, she had been doing long-distance triathlons for over a decade. She was a badass. The hill seemed long and steep, even as I drove it in my truck. I couldn't imagine the strength and determination it must have taken to ride it on a bike. But she did, just like she got through her own divorce, from Dad. The thought of her courage brought a warmth to my heart, as did the caffeine that was kicking in. I would be seeing her in less than forty-eight hours. That thought brought a big smile to my face.

I reached the top of the pass as the clouds, that had lingered throughout the day, cleared. The darkness of the night was softened by a brilliant moon, which illuminated the surrounding mountains. For the first time in a long time, I was in love with the present moment. I was grateful to have the empty highway to myself. A feeling of love rushed over me, as I made my way through the mountains towards the coast.

The next morning, I awoke in my Vancouver condo. I had arrived late the night before and had a fitful sleep. It was Christmas Eve. I lay in bed for several minutes. I was enjoying the soreness that existed throughout my entire body, after a challenging week in the backcountry. Eventually I climbed out of bed to get started on a long to-do list, that needed to be completed before my flight the next morning.

I managed to get though a full day of emails, unpacking, repacking, and cleaning. The final stop of the day was at Whole Foods, to get something for dinner. The store was full of holiday energy; families were filling their carts for a Christmas Eve feast. I was exhausted, looking to pick up something fast and easy, then head home for a dinner for one. A bachelor Christmas Eve, that was something new for me. I had been doing my best to distract myself with activities to get through the month, but no matter what I did, I could not stop Christmas from coming. I paid for a pre-packaged turkey dinner, then started the walk back home along West 7th.

Back at the condo, I checked off the last items from my list and finished packing. I had arranged a taxi pickup for early Christmas morning, so I had to get everything in order. When I was done, I heated up the pre-packaged dinner in the microwave, opened a bottle of wine, then sat down to my Christmas Eve dinner. Absent from my day was any communication with my wife. It was surreal not to hear from her at Christmas, but this was our new reality. Just then my phone buzzed with an incoming text message. A part of me hoped it was her, but I should have known better. The text was my father: "enjoy the magic of the season."

"I'll try," I wrote back. But in that moment, I just wanted the day to end.

The alarm came early Christmas morning. I showered, dressed and was in a taxi within thirty minutes. The streets were quiet as we made the drive along Granville Street toward the airport. Since I was catching one of the first flights of the day, the airport was relatively tranquil. I passed through security without issue; everyone was in a festive mood. Once onboard the plane, I took my window seat and was back asleep before the plane even took off.

I was exhausted. Not just from the last forty-eight hours of travel, unpacking, repacking, but from it all. The last two months of having my world turned upside down had drained me. My life had existed in a tumbling struggle of trying to figure out what went wrong, getting through each day, then working towards what to do next; it was all so new, so hard.

On top of it all, I was experiencing great moments of clarity, a heightened awareness. I was processing thoughts like never before. It was at times, exciting, at other times, immensely heavy. The most agonizing realizations were the ones that made me aware of the parts of my personality that I didn't want to carry forward. The self-serving, the big ego, the lack of empathy, it was those realizations that made the pain in my chest—another growing concern—tighten even further. I had another doctor's appointment booked for early in the new year, this time for a CT scan. I was getting desperate to learn the source of this ongoing discomfort in my body.

When I woke up, the plane was more than halfway across the continent. From my window seat, I looked down on a frozen Lake Michigan, some thirty thousand feet below. It looked beautiful locked in its icy winter cover.

I swiped through the touchscreen on the seatback of the chair in front of me, to choose from the music options. I usually avoided the corny compilations but somehow, I landed on a playlist with songs titled: "Honesty", "Integrity", "Connection", "Love", "Humility", "Knowledge", and "Perspective". The track titles spoke to me, especially the first one. The names of the songs summarized the values that I had been evaluating in my life over the last two months. So much had happened; I was grateful to be on a plane headed home, listening to the peaceful music. The music danced through my mind as I once again closed my eyes. I rested throughout the remainder of the flight. I felt my energy returning, and with it, the excitement of having Christmas dinner with my family that night.

A couple of hours later the plane landed in Toronto. Due to frigid temperatures and blowing snow, it looked more like the North Pole. My first stop after exiting the plane was to check the overhead screens and the status of my next flight: Flight Delayed, read the screen. "Ugh, here we go," I said to myself. With any luck the delay would be short, and I could still make Christmas dinner; a dinner that more than any other year, I now desperately wanted to be a part of. With time to spare I made my way to a restaurant in the terminal for a beer and a snack.

After I finished, I headed downstairs to the small section of the terminal with the gates for the shorter flights within Ontario. I located my gate for the one-hour flight, that would fly northeast along Lake Ontario to Kingston. Arriving at the gate, I glanced again at the overhead screen, which now read: Flight Cancelled. Staring up at the words on the screen, the weight of my bags, as well as the heaviness of the past two months, froze me in place. There would be no Christmas dinner. I did the only thing I could in that moment: breathe.

As other flights were cancelled, the small corner of the terminal was filled with enraged travellers, cursing out their displeasure. I appeared destined for Christmas dinner with an angry mob. The airline started passing out food vouchers, so a small group from my flight gathered at the nearby bar.

I took a seat next to a fellow passenger who appeared to be one of the few handling the change of plans in a state of calm. The man appeared to be in his early thirties and had a jolly disposition. I wondered, was the real-life Santa Claus, here among us? I soaked in his Zen energy, as we helped a young single mother juggle bags while balancing her baby in her arms.

In the same moment, a couple entered the corner of the small bar where we were seated. They had their hands all over each other; it was obvious they had enjoyed more than a few holiday drinks on their previous flight. They were not fazed by the change in travel plans—they had each other and there was nowhere else they needed to be. After a few of us introduced ourselves, the couple proudly shared about joining the mile-high club earlier in the day. "The best part was, we did it on the short twenty-minute flight between Nanaimo and Vancouver!" the man explained.

"Ha-ha, outstanding!" I said, as the mood amongst our motley crew began to lift.

Rumours started to circulate that the airline was arranging a bus to take our stranded souls to Kingston. With no sign of any immediate activity, I continued to order drinks with my Christmas crew. The jolly young fellow continued to calm the crowd, while helping the single mom. He shared that he was a military man, who had likely been in far more strenuous situations. His positivity, calmness, and leadership were notable.

I started talking with a stylish man, seated along the bar to my left. He began to tell me about his life together with his beautiful wife. Loosened by the alcohol, I let slip that, "I used to have a wife; that used to be me."

He responded with a consoling gaze, that made my eyes tear up. "It's probably for the better," he offered. We clinked our glasses in a silent toast, to what was turning out to be a memorable Christmas Day.

Eventually the group of a dozen Kingston-bound travellers boarded a minibus from the Toronto airport. The bus ride was subdued; we were all relieved to be moving towards our final destination. After arriving in Kingston, I caught a taxi to Mom's house. It was just before midnight when the taxi pulled off the highway onto her street. "You can just let me out here, I think I'm going to walk the rest of the way," I said, to the driver.

"Are you sure? It's freezing out there, man." asked the driver.

"Yeah, I'm good."

After paying the driver and wishing him a Merry Christmas, I started the half kilometer walk to Mom's. The sky had cleared after the snow earlier in the day. The stars in the cold sky were vivid as I made my way along the darkened road; the only sound was the squeak of the snow under my boots. After a hectic day, and a difficult two months, the stillness of the night was calming.

Despite the late hour, I was greeted by Mom as I opened the front door. "Welcome home, sweetie," she said, giving me a big hug. In that moment all my troubles disappeared; I could always trust that her love would always be present.

———————

I started Boxing Day with yoga practice. Yoga had been a part of my life for years; it was the perfect connection between the body, the mind and the breath. I set up my mat downstairs looking out on to a perfect winter landscape along the St. Lawrence River. Lying on my back in the Shavasana pose after the practice, I drifted off in a meditative state. Was it all a dream? Christmas Day, the nightmare of the last two months, the years since I left home for the West Coast, only to end up back here where it all began? I wondered if it was all a dream, then what dream would come next? My thoughts were interrupted by licks on my face by a large Italian mastiff. Sensing that Mom had sent the dog down to check on me, I was not surprised to see her coming down the stairs soon after. "Everything okay down here?" she asked.

"Yes, Mother," I muttered.

"Okay, just checking. I'm going to make something to eat. Are you hungry?"

"Absolutely. I'll be up soon."

I knew she wanted to ask more. How was I really doing? What the hell had happened? Where was Rebecca? But I was her son, so she knew I didn't want to get into it, at least not yet. No one in our family was particularly good at asking the hard questions, let alone answering them. We both knew enough details would come out in time. We also knew that sometimes just being in each other's presence was the best we could do. How could I know at the time, that my separation would bring us closer together and in the months and years that followed, we would slowly get better at communicating as a family.

After brunch, we gathered by the living room fireplace for a belated Christmas gift exchange. Mom and I were joined by her partner, Peter. My younger sister Jane, along with her partner Travis and their newborn baby, were also in town. They had made the short drive from Ottawa on Christmas Day. "Here sweetie, these are for you," said Mom, handing me a gift-wrapped package.

"Books!" I guessed, shaking the package.

"Oh, stop it, just open them," she said.

I did as I was told and removed the wrapping from the package.

Inside I found two books, as expected. I took a quick flip through the pages, which contained works of poetry, by Rupi Kaur.

"Um, what the heck—are you sure these are for me?" I asked.

"They're supposed to be good!" Mom pleaded.

"What the heck is this, Mom?!" I howled, as I flipped through the books, laughing hysterically.

In addition to the vulnerable poetry, the pencil drawings also gave me a shock. "Look at this one!" I said, as I showed everyone the drawing of a woman with her legs spread, with an accompanying poem that read: "I want to honeymoon myself."

"Did you even open these books, Mom?!" I roared with laughter, "How are these appropriate for your son?"

"Oh, for Pete sakes, Michael; she's Canadian—a rising poet—just read them, you may learn something," said Mom.

"Okay, Mother, if you say so."

The next day I made a half hour drive with Jane and her family, down the St. Lawrence River to meet Dad and his partner, Monica, for lunch. We arrived to see Dad's wood-walled bungalow covered by the recent snow fall; it looked like the perfect Christmas scene. Once inside, Dad's love of knickknacks, mementos and family photos gave the place a cabin-like feel.

After lunch, Jane started to get nervous when her two-week-old baby started to act up. She and Travis quickly gathered their belongings; they were going to have to make an early exit to drive back to their home in Ottawa. "He'll be more comfortable back home, I hope," Jane explained.

As Travis collected their mountain of baby gear, Jane quietly disappeared into a bedroom. Eventually she emerged with the heaviest tears I had ever seen run down her face. "I am so sorry we have to leave early, you came all this way," she sobbed.

"You have nothing to be sorry for, Janie," I said, as we hugged in the middle of the kitchen.

"But you flew all the way across the country to see us. I wish we could stay longer," she said.

"It's fine Jane, we got a short visit. It was perfect," I said.

We released our hug and her tears subsided. She knew I'd been through hell; she just wanted to spend more time together. She and Travis gathered their gear and headed to the door with their baby. As they made their way to their car, I realized this was why I came home: to feel the love from those who cared the most for me. It was a beautiful moment.

Later that same night, I met up with a crew of friends at the Red House Bar in downtown Kingston. A local favourite, the high wood-beamed ceilings and limestone walls were a warm retreat from the frigid outdoors. The crew gathered along one of the long tables in front of the bar. It was no small feat to bring everyone together. A whole network of babysitters had been deployed so my friends with kids could make it out. I couldn't help thinking that perhaps that extra effort was to see me and make sure I was okay. After drinks were served, I jumped into retelling the story of the books Mom had given me for Christmas: "You should have seen the drawings!" I snickered to my friends.

The unspoken was slowly addressed after several rounds of beer. Pete, the Best Man at my wedding, pulled me aside. "You know, I would do anything for you," he said.

"I know buddy," I replied.

"I was seconds away from getting on a plane to fly out west to see you," he added with tears in his eyes. "I love you, man, we all do, you'll get through this."

"I know, I love you guys too," I said. "It just... it just fucking sucks."

"I can't even imagine."

"Wow, you never see them out," said my friend Will, joining Pete and me. He was referring to Brooke and Seb, who typically avoided these holiday booze-fests. Will didn't know my news; the time hadn't been right to share. But the girls did, and I knew that's why they came out that night. It meant everything to me to have them there.

Seb was as real as they came. Faced with Leukemia and the sobering possibility of an early death, she was forced into her own life-changing adversity in her teenage years. She was also home for the holidays to visit her family. From where she now lived in Germany, she continued to be an inspiration and a shining light through her passion of writing.

"I am so happy we have reconnected," she beamed to me once we found a moment away from the others.

"Me too. I totally regret not staying better in touch over the past decade," I said.

"I feel the same way."

"Do you think it was a lost decade for us, as friends?" I asked.

"Not at all, everything happens for a reason. Our journeys took us on different paths," she answered.

"It's good to be home, isn't it?" I asked.

"Yeah, it sure is. So, how are you? What happened?" she asked.

"I'm okay. I'll be okay. We...well I guess we just drifted apart. The shitty part is she never gave us a real chance to make it work, she just made her decision and that was it. It totally sucks."

"That's so hard. I'm so sorry Mike; you don't deserve this."

"Thank you, no one deserves this; but I guess that's life though, you know all about that, don't you?"

"I sure do," she said, smiling.

Soon after people slowly started to leave the bar. Most of the parents had to get home to relieve their babysitters. After a couple more drinks, Brooke and I were two of the last people in the bar. "Thanks for helping to convince me to come home," I said, reminding her of the texts she sent earlier in the month.

"You're very welcome. I know what's good for ya," she said.

"Ya, you and my mother."

"So, what the hell happened between you and Rebecca?"

"Well," I sighed, feeling the influence of the alcohol, "I guess she just wanted to live a different life, without me."

"Ah shit, so sorry, dude."

"Thanks, bud. How have you been?"

"Just surviving, raising two kids. It can be a lot at times."

"I can't even imagine. Maybe I'll know one day, if I'm lucky, that is."

"You will, buddy. You'll be a great dad."

"Ya, I hope so, but it's kind of hard to think about that now."

"Ya, no doubt, one day at a time."

"Let's get out of here, this place is done," I said, referring to the emptying bar.

"Sounds good to me."

We gathered our coats, scarves, and hats in preparation to enter the polar vortex that was waiting outside. Once dressed, we made our way to the exit. Upon opening the door to the outside, we were instantly greeted with a blast of the frigid minus twenty-five-degree Celsius air. We walked the half block over to the main street with hopes of quickly finding a taxi to share. Of course, being a small town, there were none to be found. "What are we going to do? It's freaking freezing out here!" I said.

"There's only one place that's open at this late hour—Tim Hortons!"

Brooke replied.

"Sounds good. Hopefully, we can call a taxi from there," I said.

A frozen five-minute walk later we entered the empty coffee shop. A lone nightshift worker greeted us. With a beauty, energy, and sense of humour that lights up every room, Brooke set to work entertaining the young male worker. "We'll have two teas and two donuts, young man!" she said, "And make it snappy, we're freezing!"

"Go easy on the young dude, Brooke!" I said.

As we waited for the teas to arrive, Brooke lovingly tormented the young worker. I reflected that this same scene, in the same coffee shop, had been replayed countless times before, back in high school. Everything had changed over the past twenty years, but at the same time, nothing had changed at all. We were still out late after a great night out, we were still hanging out with our same friends, we were still laughing at the same stupid jokes. The only difference was twenty years' worth of memories; some good, some far from it.

Eventually I got through to the taxi company and secured our ride home. Brooke was staying at her parents' house near my mom's, so we shared the ride. As I got out of the taxi at the end of Mom's road for my new ritual walk, Brooke called out from the taxi, "You should come visit Toronto for a night this weekend when I am back there. It would be a blast!"

"Not possible, my friend, I'm flying back to Vancouver in two days."

"Bummer, dude, next time!"

The invitation felt good, but I didn't give it much thought on my frigid walk down the desolate road. As I walked, I stared up into the deep black sky. The sky was filled with frozen stars a million miles away. I was alone again; I felt like my only companion in that moment was the light breeze rattling the frozen tree limbs that lined the dark road. The return to feeling lonely, after a day of family and friends, brought frozen tears to my cheeks. The love I felt on that day had distracted me from my pain. As I walked, my mind drifted towards my unknown future. Anxiety grew within me, thinking about facing the new year alone. I had to learn how to better maintain that feeling of love in the present moment, instead of getting overwhelmed worrying about the future. I had to learn how to better control my thoughts.

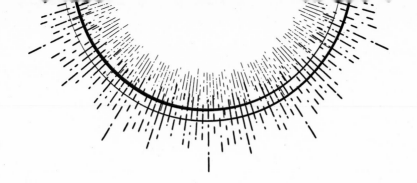

CHAPTER 5

NEW YEAR, NEW ME

I love the man that can smile in trouble, that can gather strength from distress, and grow brave by reflection.

THOMAS PAINE

My headache woke me early the next morning. My first thought was questioning if I was dehydrated from the alcohol, or all the tears. My second thought was that I was getting tired of the seemingly perpetual hungover version of myself. I had never been a huge drinker, but I had always suffered bad headaches the morning after. The hangovers had gotten worse with each passing year. Despite the sometimes debilitating pain, I continued to drink like I was years younger. I had never thought of myself as having a drinking 'problem', but I was feeling pulled to step into a new version of me.

Lifting my head from the pillow, I reached over and dug through my bag for the Advil I knew I would need on the trip. The pain in my head was too great for a return to sleep, so instead, I journaled about the events from the day before.

Once the thoughts were out of my head and my headache started to subside, I slowly crawled out of bed. Outside my bedroom, I shuffled across the cold tile floor and made my way to the kitchen. Looking out of the windows beyond the snowy backyard, Milton Island seemed to float among the steam rising off the river. All the heat was being sucked out of the water, as it turned to ice. The first hints of light rose with the sun across the distant shores on Wolfe Island.

Mom was already in the kitchen, so I joined her for some much-needed coffee. "You were out late, sweetie," Mom observed, just as she had a thousand times before.

"Ugh, my head," I grunted.

"Oh Michael, when will you learn?"

"But we have fun."

"Ya but look at you. And you stink like booze, too!"

"Blah, I know. Coffee please."

My phone vibrated as I guzzled the coffee. "Who's that at this early hour?" asked Mom.

"It's a text from the airline about my flight tomorrow, it can't be good."

"Maybe your flight will be cancelled again, and you can stay longer with me!"

"It says it's just delayed. How can they know that a day in advance? Whatever, I'll deal with it later."

"Sounds good, honey, more coffee?"

"Please."

Later in the day I received a second text about a further delay.

I started to consider that perhaps the Universe was trying to tell me something; I gave a second thought to Brooke's suggestion of a night in Toronto with friends. After a call to the airline a new plan was formed: I would take the reliable train from Kingston to Toronto, spend the night with friends, then fly out to Vancouver the next day.

I felt completely drained rolling out of town on the train twenty-four hours later. The whirlwind trip to Kingston, the late nights out, the emotion of seeing everyone—I carried all of it with me onto the train. It was a little over two hours to get to Toronto, so I opened my laptop to catch up on work emails, organize photos from the first ski trip, and coordinate food arrangements for the second, upcoming ski trip next week back in BC. At the same time, I was on my cell phone getting directions from Brooke for my arrival in Toronto, texting with other friends, and posting my thoughts on social media from my time spent in Kingston. Fuelled by a tinfoil-wrapped leftover turkey sandwich—a staple parting gift from Mom—I entered a state of hyper focus, organizing my life so I could be fully present with friends once I arrived in Toronto.

As I stepped out of the train, I was hit with a blast of cold air on the platform at Union Station. I moved through the station and out onto Front Street, where I could feel the energy of the big city, amplified by it being a Friday night during the holidays. I hailed a taxi without difficulty. Once inside, I shared Brooke's meticulous directions, as I finished the last of my sandwich. After picking up Brooke and stopping at a liquor store, we arrived at my friend Jeremy's house.

Jeremy lived in a three-story Victorian brick walk-up, in an area of Toronto known as Cabbagetown. Across the street from his house was a snow-filled park lit by soft light from perfectly spaced lamp posts. The streets were lined with wide snowbanks, leaving room for only one car at a time. The parked cars were covered with snow; it looked as though some hadn't moved at all during the holidays. I had no idea such a quaint area existed within the big city. It reminded me of the neighbourhood in Kingston where I grew up.

Inside, the vibe was just as good: drinks were flowing, music was playing, and a real wood fire warmed the space. I hadn't spoken to Jeremy since the night of The National concert, earlier in the month. It was good to see him in person. His wife, and childhood friend of mine, Sarah, was able to coordinate a few others to come over at the last minute. Our friend Alex arrived, as did Sarah's older brothers Darren and Mike, along with Mike's wife and newborn baby.

We pushed through several bottles of wine over the course of the evening. I had been drinking way too much, as had the others. I convinced myself that the time spent with friends was too good to pass up. This was what we had done for years, this was how we spent our time together, and I wouldn't trade it for the world. The hangovers, they were a different story; I could have lived without those. Eventually we called it a night when the wine ran out. I dragged myself upstairs to a spare bedroom to catch a few hours of sleep.

I woke up early the next morning to maximize my short time in the city. Brooke, who also spent the night at Jeremy's, was up early as well. We made our way towards Parliament Street and some much-needed caffeine to tame our headaches. As we made our way through the neighbourhood, I was amazed that this pocket of Toronto had eluded me for years. Having grown up only a couple of hours away in Kingston, I had spent many weekends visiting Toronto. Still, I had never spent time in this area. We entered a coffee shop on Parliament. Much to my delight, it was decorated with a theme of different vintage road-biking art forms. "This is where the local road bikers gather in the warmer months, after their rides," Brooke said.

"This is amazing. Who knew?! I could live here," I said, as we placed our orders. This is what she had shown me: that I could live and be happy somewhere other than Vancouver. This realization was exciting, as it opened a whole new realm of possibilities for what my future could look like, now that the likely end of the marriage meant I was no longer tied to Vancouver. At the same time, this ultimate freedom to move somewhere new, was overwhelming and a lot to process.

"These guys travel around the world on road biking trips, but still live and work here in Toronto," Brooke said, as we found an empty table.

She was showing me that it was possible to still do the sports that I loved so much: the skiing, the surfing, the biking, without having to live in Vancouver. Maybe I could explore a world outside of my familiar reality and still do the activities that made my heart race. Maybe I could have more new experiences in new places to further awaken my brain, like what I'd felt on that visit to Toronto. The possibilities were invigorating, or perhaps it was the caffeine, or lack of sleep. Either way, by seeing and feeling this new experience, in a new place, I was beginning to see how it could be possible to create a future life that was different from what I had lived in the past. If that was what I desired. I still had to get clear on that part.

Once we were done at the coffee shop, I walked Brooke back to her place a few blocks away and called a taxi to take me to the airport. The taxi arrived soon after. We said our goodbyes and I thanked her again for her persistence in getting me to come home. "You're a real pain in the ass, you know?" I joked to her, as I got into the taxi.

"I just know what's best for ya, buddy," she called out, as I closed the door and we started to drive away.

As the taxi made its way through the city, I stared out the window as the grey buildings passed by. I reflected on my short, but intense visit. Tears started to fill my eyes as I thought about the memories over the past few days: the Christmas Day travel drama, that first hug from Mom when I finally made it home, my sister's big tears when she had to leave early, the night out with everyone at the Red House, the solitude of my nightly frozen walks, and now this new experience in Toronto. For the first time in two months I smiled as I cried; finally, I was crying tears of joy.

The taxi arrived at the airport and I made my way through security without issue. The plane was on time, so I went straight to the gate and boarded after a short wait. As the plane took off and pointed to the west, I closed my eyes for a power nap.

I jolted awake twenty minutes later. I opened my eyes and looked out the window and thought back on the year in which everything changed. From the outside the change was obvious, with the breakup. But something else had changed, within me. I was feeling and thinking on a new level of consciousness. I was self-analyzing every aspect of my personality and taking the sometimes painful ownership of parts I wanted to improve. I was hungry to explore new perspectives and have my mindset shifted. The more I learned, the more I became aware of how little I knew. I was operating from a place that I never knew existed. I had to capture this powerful transformation that was taking place; I had to acknowledge this change in a meaningful and permanent way. I took a deep breath as I watched the clouds stream by below the plane.

It became clear to me how I would do this; I would follow through on something I'd always wanted, but never had the courage to do: I would get a tattoo. But a tattoo of what?

For years I'd toyed with the idea of a tattoo. I'd thought of getting some sort of west coast scene, showing my love and connection with nature. I'd envisioned three mountains, the tallest in the middle, all with exposed rocky peaks, rising above a thick forest below. At the base of the mountain a narrow channel would grow to a larger body of water. But how to also capture my transformation?

When I had been waiting at the gate for the flight to board, I had read online about *Unalomes*: symbols which represent the journey to reach enlightenment. A Unalome consists of a line rising from the centre of a spiral. The line goes through additional smaller spirals before reaching a straight line out the top, symbolizing enlightenment. As you move up from the bottom spiral, you become more conscious of your surroundings, of your journey. The spirals signify how everyone's journey is different and full of many twists and turns. The bottom spiral, larger than the others, represents the journey inward, that we must first take before we truly know ourselves. From that journey we can proceed up the path to enlightenment, with more power and wisdom to share and help others.

After my memorable trip home, I also wanted to acknowledge my deep connection to my hometown, Kingston. That symbol was obvious: Gord Downie. Gord was the lead singer of The Tragically Hip, one of Canada's greatest rock bands, who also happened to be based in Kingston. I grew up listening to the band, obsessing over their albums, running into band members around town. Gord was my hero. As I grew older, I began to appreciate the lyrics and the lessons that he wove into his songs. He wrote passionately about Canadian issues and became a national icon in the process. When he was diagnosed with terminal brain cancer, the entire country was affected. Miraculously, despite his diagnosis, the band performed one last tour across Canada, to bless their fans with a final act. Gord died only weeks before my separation. It was as though I was forced to let go of multiple parts of my former life at the same time.

Thinking back, I recalled the style of hat that Gord wore during his final tour with The Tragically Hip; it had a round brim with a distinctive feather sticking out of one side. With the image in my mind, I pulled my journal out of my bag and tried to bring the elements together: the mountains, trees, water, Unalome, and Gord's hat. The resulting sketch could only be described as a true disaster—I could not draw to save my life. The sketch resembled three triangles, a loose dangling string, and a deformed leprechaun's hat. It would not do. Surely a professional would be able to bring my vision to life.

———————

The next morning, I woke up back in my Vancouver condo. It was New Year's Eve. My first thoughts went to the memories of the whirlwind trip to Ontario. Next, I thought ahead with anxiety to all the packing I had to do before leaving for another ski trip the next day. (A truly first-world privileged problem.) Finally, the heaviness of this new state of feeling at extremes began to weigh on my mind. With hopes of reducing the stress of bouncing my thoughts between the painful past and the uncertain future, I vowed to make only one resolution for the coming year: be present.

When I was in the present moment, like during the times in Kingston when I was out with my friends, or when I was walking in solitude to Mom's, I had feelings of radiant joy. During these times there was no place I'd rather be. I lacked for nothing in those moments. All the pain from the past and worry of the future, simply did not exist. When living fully in the present moment, I could exist in a state of bliss.

Lying in bed on the last day of 2017, I opened *The Untethered Soul,* the book my counselor had recommended to help me better understand the connection between my thoughts and who I was. I had been reading it on the plane the previous day, and had dogeared a page with a powerful passage:

> *"You are not your thoughts; you are aware of your thoughts.*
> *You are not your emotions; you feel your emotions.*
> *You are not your body; you look at it in the mirror and experience the world through its eyes and ears.*
> *You are the conscious being who is aware that you are aware of all these inner and outer things."*

I closed the book after reading the passage. Who was I? The book was saying that I was not my past, my pain, my thoughts, my body. Rather I was a consciousness that was aware of all these things. How could that be? I had always assumed that I was defined by my thoughts and past experiences. Now I was learning that what I thought, was not necessarily who I was. Rather, I was the one aware of my thoughts; I was a conscious being, aware that I was aware of my thoughts. I wondered, what the heck did that even mean? Did it mean that if my thoughts were of darkness and being alone, that I was not these things, but that I was the one who was aware that I was aware of these thoughts? I struggled with the concept; it was a lot to process, especially after the busyness of the last few weeks. I resolved to dig deeper in the new year, to better understand the concept, and to better understand myself. But first, I had a ton of packing to do.

Just like a week earlier, the day passed in a blur of unpacking, laundry, repacking, and grocery shopping. I was scheduled to leave on this second ski trip the next day, New Year's Day. The trips were serving as a perfect distraction to the suffering I was still feeling from the separation. Subconsciously, I was worried about what was going to happen when the travel came to an end, and I returned to my normal working life. But in that moment, the full pace was me at my best: the travel, the action, the movement, it's what fueled my soul.

After a long day of chores, I returned to the condo to address the final big question of the year: how to spend New Year's Eve? I pondered the question over a big glass of red wine, while staring at the bright city lights through the living room window. I debated making the short walk over the Granville Bridge, to take in New Year's at a friend's condo party. It was an annual gathering. The number of guests had been dwindling over the years, as more couples chose to stay home; some had new babies to care for. The rest of the crowd would be predictable, the same conversations, the same jokes, and the same random shots of booze.

I didn't want to go but felt like I should leave the condo and be with other humans on New Year's Eve. Wasn't that what I was supposed to do? But if I did go, who was I supposed to kiss at midnight? For the first time in years, I'd be alone. The thought wasn't inspiring me to attend the soiree. Instead, I poured a second glass of red.

Standing in the middle of the condo, I stared at the Christmas lights hung around the living room window. The stereo pumped with rhythmic beats. My mind swirled with each sip of wine. I walked over to the dining room table and picked up the other book I had been reading recently: Eckart Tolle's *A New Earth*[2]. The book was first recommended to me by Max, years ago. I had tried to read it back then but understood very little. In the past month, I had revisited the book with hopes of better understanding Tolle's teachings on awareness, consciousness, and our thoughts. I opened the book to a passage I had recently highlighted:

> *"All things are vibrating energy fields in ceaseless motion. Thoughts consist of the same energy, vibrating at a higher frequency than matter, which is why they can't be seen or touched."*

I thought back to November and the fateful night at Barney's with Jeff and Kelsey. I remembered Jeff saying, "Thoughts are only vibration." At the time I had no clue what he was talking about. Now I was getting closer, but still grasping to fully understand the connection between thoughts and energy. Tolle was saying that thoughts are the same type of energy as all other things, but they are vibrating at a higher frequency, so we can't see them. Thoughts are made up with the same energy as say, a chair, except the energy fields in a chair vibrate at a lower frequency, and that's why we can see the chair. Whereas thoughts vibrate at higher frequencies and are therefore invisible to the human eye. The concept made me think of wireless internet. No one could see it, but we all know it exists.

I was getting close to being able to visualize this, but what was the point? What did it all mean? If thoughts were just energy, how could

---

2 Tolle, Eckhart. *A New Earth: Awakening to Your Life's Purpose.* Penguin Life, 2008.

we tap into that energy to control and direct our thoughts? Was it possible to control our energy and therefore control our thoughts? Could this be the way out of the thoughts of loneliness and despair that I was still carrying at times? My mind raced with these questions. I took another sip of wine; I had to explore these thoughts more.

I read further and came across the story of the Zen Master and the quote:

> "*Nonresistance, nonjudgement, and nonattachment are the three aspects of true freedom and enlightened living.*"

Was that all it took? By adopting these three aspects into my life could I experience true freedom and enlightened living? Could I alter my perspective and accept that my present situation was temporary and would eventually pass? Could I achieve freedom from the suffering that lingered in my mind by not resisting or judging challenging situations as they came up? It seemed so simple. But if it was so simple, why wouldn't everyone think like this and set themselves free? I poured another glass and acknowledged that I wouldn't be heading out to celebrate New Year's, I was already having too good a time.

I continued to read on. My mind began to wander, thinking about how great a life of true freedom and enlightened living could be. Then I read the word: *satori*. It was a Japanese Buddhist term for awakening; it meant a flash of enlightenment. I'd never seen the word before. It pulled me in. I loved how it sounded, how it felt, and most of all, what it meant. It represented acquiring a new point of view and moving through life with a greater understanding and comprehension, moving closer towards our true selves, living in alignment with our purpose. Was this happening to me, I wondered. Did this one word describe all my feelings, emotions, and experiences that were unlocked in the trauma of the breakup?

I continued to read and came across a second word: *ananda*. Ananda was Sanskrit; it represented the bliss of being. I said it over and over to myself. I loved how it rolled off my tongue, ananda, bliss, one of the highest states of being. The word reminded me of the joy and happiness I felt when living fully in the present moment. Sitting at the dining room table, I leaned back in my chair and gazed skyward. I breathed in the power of these two words. Two words I had serendipitously discovered to help explain all I was going through. I radiated gratitude as I whispered these two words, my two words, *satori ananda*.

Despite feeling drained from the day, I decided to push on and make it to midnight. I had to make a decision on how I wanted to ring in New Year's: peacefully in bed reflecting on the past twelve months, lying on the living room carpet journaling my thoughts, or out on the balcony with the sounds of fireworks from across the city.

I chose to go outside on the balcony to film the fireworks on my phone. I made my way outside just before twelve o'clock. At the stroke of midnight, the entire city came together with a chorus of horns honking, fireworks exploding, and shouts of joy. I filmed it all and felt the energy of the celebration pulse through my body. The celebration lasted only a few minutes, and I returned to the warmth of the living room to watch the video I had just recorded. What I saw on the screen would be something I would never forget: as the clock struck midnight, the city erupted and every light in the downtown core appeared to flicker on and off. It was as though every person was purposely switching their lights on and off. At the same time, the noise from the celebration grew to a crescendo. This explosion of light, sound and energy continued for the full video.

I tried to comprehend what I was seeing, as this was not what I witnessed live moments ago. The replay on my phone looked like a movie scene. What I saw in person on the deck was just the odd firework exploding and lots of cheering. I accepted that the video was just some distortion within my phone's camera. But still, there was something about that video; there was something magical going on.

After the excitement wore off, I eventually went to bed. It had turned out to be a memorable New Year's Eve, even though I was alone in my condo. I realized that even though I had spent the night alone, I had never felt lonely. I thought back to the love that I had felt from so many over the past two months, love that surely lingered in spirit within my home that night. I was grateful. "Thank you, Universe," I whispered to myself. "Thank you for all the love; thank you for all that you have shown me." As I drifted off to sleep, I knew that the scene on my phone was the entire city, the entire Universe, cheering me on as I continued down a new path, towards a new me.

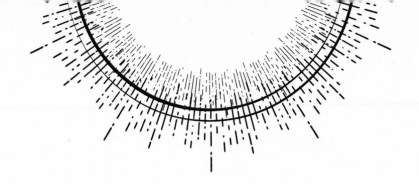

CHAPTER 6

HIGHER HIGHS, LOWER LOWS

If you're going through hell, keep going.

WINSTON CHURCHILL

Had I seen God? That was my first thought waking up on New Year's Day. I wasn't religious, but my beliefs, like everything else, had evolved over the previous months. Considering the events that had occurred during this time, and the new awareness that I was developing, I landed on a new perspective: there must be a higher power connecting us all; there must be something greater than the individual; there must be something unleashing the highs of my revelations; there must be something putting me through the painful lows, there must be a greater purpose to it all. That was no small realization for a groggy New Year's Day.

After pulling myself out of bed and making an espresso, I took a seat at the dining room table. To start the new year, I wrote out several of Tolle's passages that I had bookmarked over the past week. I focused on one of my favourites:

> *"Not what you do, but how you do what you do determines whether you are fulfilling your destiny."*

"How you do what you do"—I repeated these words as I gazed at the condo towers through the living room windows. The city was quiet, compared to last night's festivities. For now, I was *doing* engineering Monday to Friday, nine to five, and for the most part, I was doing it well. Was that it? Was that what I was put on this earth to do? Was that me living my purpose? After twelve years, it sure didn't feel like it. Either way, it paid well; it helped pay for my condo, the ski trip before Christmas and the upcoming ski trip—a trip with a different group of friends, in a different part of the province, that I desperately needed to finish packing for.

Later that afternoon I drove east out of Vancouver and into the Coast Mountains. I was heading for dinner in Kamloops with Max. Halfway through the drive I pulled over just past the Coquihalla summit. The view was breathtaking. The snowbanks were fifteen feet high and contrasted beautifully against the blue sky and white mountain peaks in the distance. I sent off a few pictures to my buddies in Ontario, poking fun at their flat landscape. After I sent the photos, I saw a new email had arrived from a tattoo artist I'd messaged about the vision I had for my design.

Expectations were high as I opened the attachment to see if she had accurately captured the concept that I could not sketch. My excitement quickly vanished as I reviewed her work: it just wasn't right. I had a vision for how it could all come together, but neither of us were able to capture it. Perhaps I was asking too much, trying to include too many components for my first tattoo. Or maybe I was trying to over validate my experiences over the past two months. Either way, there was nothing I could do about the sketch. I was about to return to the backcountry for a week, where I would be off the grid. The tattoo quandary would eventually sort itself out. I hoped.

I arrived shortly before dinner time at Max's house in Kamloops. It was the first time seeing him in person since the separation. It was also the first time seeing his partner, Romina, who happened to be Rebecca's best friend. I entered the kitchen of their small house on Pine Street through the backyard. Sarge, their dog, was the first to greet me, followed by Max right behind him. "You made it!" said Max, as he gave me a hug.

"I always do, brother. Happy New Year, man," I said.

"Happy New Year," said Max.

"Hi Mikey. It's good to see you," said Romina, entering the kitchen.

"Good to see you too, Romina," I said, giving her a hug and putting any unease to rest.

It was awkward to be there without Rebecca. The four of us had been an adventuring team for years. We spent countless couple's weekends camping, doing wine tours, or skiing. It had been perfect. But now that Max and Romina had a baby and Rebecca and I were no longer together, things had changed.

After I washed up, Max and I headed out to get some dinner. Romina stayed behind with their baby. New Year's Day dinner options in small-town Kamloops were near non-existent—most restaurants were closed. We managed to find the only place open in a strip mall in the middle of town. "Man, I am so looking forward to this. I could use a little guy time," Max said, as we parked.

"Ya, man, me too. Lots to chat about," I said.

"Oh ya, you've got to fill me in on what's been going on with you. The writing you shared with me, and the stuff you've been posting, man, that's some deep stuff," Max said.

"I'll tell you all about it. Let's get inside, it's freezing out here."

The restaurant was near empty, so we chose an oversized booth on the far side of the bar. "Amazing, some customers!" said the server, approaching our table.

"Where the heck is everyone in this town?" I asked.

"Beats me, people must have gone too hard last night. What'll it be boys?" she said.

"Two pale ales to get us started," I said.

"Coming right up," she said, as she turned back towards the bar.

"I saw that you were posting stuff on social media about Tolle's writing. You've been reading him again?" asked Max.

"Ya man. Remember when you first recommended *A New Earth* to me a couple years ago?"

"Sure do, I've always said that it was my bible."

"Well, I read it back then, and barely understood any of his concepts. Being present, the ego, pain bodies, it all went over my head."

"Well, ya, it's heavy stuff. There is nothing else like it out there."

"I'm rereading it now and I feel like I understand ninety-five percent of it. It's crazy. It's so good."

"Dude! That's amazing. I'm jealous!"

The beer arrived and we placed our orders for food. I shared about my plans for the next few months. "I'll do this ski trip this week—which should be epic—then head back to Vancouver. After that I'll be on standby to head over to Victoria for a project."

"How long will you be over there?"

"Should be about three months, so maybe until the end of April or so."

"Then what?"

"I don't know. Maybe I'll take some time off and go traveling."

"Can you do that with your work? Would they let you?"

"I don't know, I've never asked. But I mean, I'll be working a ton of extra hours in Victoria, so I should have some leverage. Plus, I could always play the breakup card."

"Ya man, have you told anyone at work?"

"Not yet, I will when I get back from this trip."

"How do you think that will go?"

"I don't know. They're usually supportive. I'm not too worried. Either way, I'm looking forward to a change by going to Victoria,"

"Ya, man, I hear ya. I could use a change too, but it's definitely harder now that we have a baby."

"I can only imagine; you'll find your groove though."

"It's good to see you. It's cool that you've started posting and sharing what you've been reading and all that you are learning."

"Ya, I've been reading so much, trying to figure out how to be happy again. It's been tough."

"I can't imagine. It'll only get better."

"Cheers, man, we'll see."

I was up early the next morning. Max was up soon after to make us both coffees before I hit the road. "Be safe out there," he said, as I made my way to the door.

As I was driving out of town, I received a text from Romina: "Seeing you makes it more real." It was true; it was more real that the separation had happened, that Rebecca had chosen another path. A decision that had an obvious effect on our relationship, but also impacted others who we were connected to. There would be no more camping trips, no more dinners with endless laughter, no more hanging out as a foursome like we did for so many years. The change was real.

I absorbed that hard truth as I made my way along the empty highway leaving Kamloops. I had plenty of time to drive north to Clearwater and meet the others before the start of the trip. On the drive I passed through an area when a forest fire had scarred the pine trees across the rolling hillside. With frigid temperatures below minus twenty Celsius and a thin cover of white snow, the blackened tree remnants looked ghostly in the early morning light. Being present with this juxtaposition of the extremes of nature made me excited to be immersed in the wild for the week ahead.

I arrived at the helicopter hangar one and a half hours later, ahead of schedule and before the others. Before going into the backcountry and losing cell service for the week, I made a few final work calls and emails. Soon my friends started to arrive. They had chosen to spend the night at a motel in Clearwater, while I had stayed with Max in Kamloops. After I finished my calls, I met the others in the hangar for a safety briefing. I arrived just after the meeting had started and took a seat off to the side.

The briefing was led by the tour operator who gave the usual rundown of expected weather, avalanche conditions and emergency procedures. The topics always demanded our respect and attention, but I could feel an extra tension in the air. For me, like the previous trip, I was nervous about being embedded in a small cabin for a week considering the rolling emotions I had been dealing with. While I was occasionally experiencing peaceful moments, when being fully present in nature, I was still struggling when my mind would drift to relive the past or I'd become anxious about the unknown future. It was during these times when my swirling thoughts took over that the tension in my chest would also grow. I seemed to be experiencing higher emotions than ever before, but with it, also came a new level of lingering sorrow. Just like the mountains and the valleys we were about to go into, I was living in a world of higher highs and lower lows. This would also be the first time I would see many from this group since the separation, so I sensed they were equally nervous to see how I was holding up.

After the briefing, we made the half-hour drive to meet the snow cat that would shuttle us into the mountains. We had all our heavy gear, as well as the food and alcohol, flown in by helicopter. We arrived safely at the cabin, a rustic A-frame, later in the afternoon. After a busy few weeks, I told the others that my main goal during the trip was to catch up on sleep. Everyone else was stoked to ski, so they headed out for a quick run while I tucked in for an alpine nap. As the last of the crew made their way out the door, I savoured the serene silence alone in the cabin. I returned to my New Year's resolution of being present.

Three days in, without any new fresh snow, I could sense the others growing anxious. The group I was with was my main crew, who I'd been skiing with for the past decade. The ten of us had shared a lot together over the years. We'd got through some tough times together, both in the mountains, and in life. I knew they were hungry, like I was, for the fresh snow and untracked powder that made these trips special.

Aware of this growing unease, I did my best to motivate the others by staying positive during the long, hard climbs back to the top of the runs. Like my previous trip, at the bottom of each run we would attach climbing skins to the base of our skis, switch our bindings into climbing mode, then start the slow ascent back to the top.

I felt strong on the climbs after my previous trip. At the start of each climb I put my headphones on and hit play on a new playlist. The playlist was loaded with the same high energy music that had fueled me back in the city. The music helped carry me to the top in a trance of beats and rhythms. I sang out loud, when I wasn't out of breath.

On our final climb of the third day, I paused halfway to look across the valley at the majestic peaks looming in the distance. In the centre of the scene rose a stunning rocky summit with a long, empty, gnarled face. With this perfect mountain rising before me, my mind wandered back to the disappointment of the tattoo artist's sketch that I had received a few days earlier. As I stood catching my breath, my thoughts drifted to New Year's Eve and the incredible night I had alone in my condo. I remembered the two words I read on that night and how they captivated me: *satori*—a flash of enlightenment, a new point of view, a greater understanding and comprehension, moving closer to our true selves, living in alignment with our purpose; *ananda*—the bliss of being, finding extreme happiness, one of the highest states of being.

In that very moment, staring across the valley, it became clear what my first tattoo would be: not an image of a rising mountain, but instead those two words: *satori ananda*. With that clarity I tilted my head to soak in the brilliant rays of alpine sunshine. I had my tattoo. Not the combination of mountains, trees, and ocean, but instead, two magical words.

Later that night I found myself alone outside in the dark at the Pee Tree. I was on a high after a night of good food, drink, and sauna. The cabin had a separate outhouse building, but the guys on the trip preferred to use the designated tree: the tree smelled better than the outhouse, and it came with the added challenge of tunneling a pee hole in the snow over the course of the week.

Since I had just left the sauna, I was only wearing a pair of crocs, a towel around my waist, and an unbuttoned plaid shirt; luckily, the Pee Tree never judged appearances. Gazing up at the trees overhead, my mind drifted back to dinner with Max in Kamloops. I focused on how good it felt to share openly with him about all I had been going through. By doing this, it seemed to give him permission to be vulnerable and share his challenges as well. This authentic conversation felt so good, and only took a little courage from both of us to admit that things in our lives were far from perfect. Looking up through the snow-covered trees at the beaming full moon overhead, I had my second realization of the day. Somewhere within this thought was my purpose in life: to share my thoughts and give others the permission to do the same, to courageously embrace vulnerability, and to help lead others to deeper and more meaningful connections. It was a mouthful and still needed some refinement, but there was something there.

My feet began to freeze as I was pulled out of my mind and back down to earth. I turned quickly to head back to the cabin and slipped, just avoiding a slide into the pee tunnel that had formed after several days of use. Laughing to myself, I regained my footing and looked into the sky once more: what was this new life? What were all these realizations? How could I learn more about these new thoughts I was having? As I approached the cabin, I decided not to share my latest revelation with the others; a revelation that I had found dressed like a half-naked lumberjack at the sacred Pee Tree.

The high was short-lived and was replaced with a painful new low the next night. After enjoying too many drinks in the sauna with the others, I walked directly into the sauna stove and seared my naked left thigh. The pain was tremendous... "Fuck me," I cursed to the others.

"Dude, get outside and put some snow on it," said one of my buddies. After cooling the burn with a handful of snow, I looked down to see a glowing red patch of skin slightly larger than a deck of cards. "Idiot," I said to myself.

I sulked off to my upstairs sleeping pad. I was disappointed in myself. On top of that, I didn't want to be on the trip anymore. The ski conditions weren't improving, and I felt like I was wasting my days. What I really wanted to be doing was learning more about this new awareness that I was developing. I wanted to see if I could somehow direct it and go further. Above all, I wanted to see if a focused awareness could help me stop sliding between these higher highs, and lower lows. I just wanted the highs. What I didn't want was this pain in my leg. I also didn't want to be drunk or hungover anymore. I wanted a clear mind so I could learn more about this change that had started within me. I needed silence, something that was not going to be possible in the tight confines of the cabin. I needed to get off this mountain. I needed to be back home in my own space, to do more work on myself.

All of this was huge change for me. In the past, I loved every moment in the mountains, whether there was fresh snow or not. I also used to be the life of the party—often one of the last people awake each night. I used to ski and party like I approached everything in life: all in. These parts of me—like most of my identity—became uncertain with the breakup. In that moment, I had bigger things to worry about: like who I really was. I thought ahead to getting off the mountain and back to my productive life back home in the city. But what would I be returning to, more highs or more lows? What was waiting for me after all these trips and distractions?

I managed to get through the last couple days of the trip by heavily wrapping my leg in gauze and medical tape. My leg hurt, but the skiing seemed to act as a distraction from the pain. I skied out to the cars on the last day with the group then made the drive back to Vancouver. A day after returning home I had my wish: I was sitting alone in the condo with only my thoughts. But I had not returned to a high.

Instead, I was sitting at the dining room table, wearing only my boxers, in a depressing new reality. I'd never felt worse. Without the distraction of the skiing, the burn on my leg seemed to pulse with a relentless throbbing. The adrenaline that had fueled me through the last few days had been replaced with a searing pain. The pain was too great to put on pants, so I was forced to stay in the condo instead of going into work. I had the silence I wanted but struggled to maintain focus. After being offline for a week, I succeeded in getting through a stack of work emails but accomplished little else—I was too busy feeling sorry for myself.

Sitting alone in the condo with my leg throbbing, my mind began to race as thoughts festered in my head. Was this how the new year was going to play out? After a hectic November and December, and a well-conceived three-week tour of distractions, I had returned to the same sad, empty, lonely condo. On top of that, I had returned with a fried leg that prevented me from doing the daily exercise that kept me sane. In those moments over the past few weeks, when I felt absolutely present in the moment, life felt like a dream. All the pain from the breakup, and the uncertainty from the future, had melted away. But those moments were short-lived and often accessed when I was immersed in nature. Was that my quota for the year? Was I to accept that I'd had my fun, and now it was back to the grind? Was that how life worked? Suffer all year round only to get a taste of the good life. My mind raced. I didn't know the answers. What I did know was that I was running out of distractions. I was going to have to figure out these racing thoughts by addressing them head on. The challenge was, I didn't know how.

The ensuing couple of days unraveled in a similar pant-less festering routine. I sent photo updates to my sister Jenn, a doctor, who advised me to keep the wound clean and be patient—something that was not my strength. While I was suffering being immobile in my condo, admittedly, I wasn't too excited to get back to my engineering office job. I wondered how long I could remain away. Despite doing good work and being well compensated over the last year, I knew in my heart that after twelve years as an engineer, it wasn't lighting my soul on fire. In my mind I committed to do my best work over the next few months once the Victoria project got underway. After that, perhaps I would take some time to reassess. I also knew that I was subconsciously avoiding the office because I was putting off telling my colleagues about the separation. I knew the time had come to at least tell my boss and share my developing plan for some time off in the spring. This was a hard conversation that had to happen soon.

Throughout the week, I skimmed through a new book I had picked up from the library, *Altered Traits*[3]. The title spoke to me. I had been searching for something to help explain the depths of the new thoughts, feelings, and awareness I was having. In the book, I read about the four healthy states of mind: even-mindedness, compassion, ongoing mindfulness, and realistic confidence. I certainly didn't have all of those going for me.

---

3 Goleman, Daniel, & Davidson, Richard J. *Altered Traits: Science Reveals How Meditation Changes Your Mind, Brain, and Body.* Avery, 2017.

The higher highs and lower lows that I was feeling seemed to be the furthest thing from even-mindedness.

I was developing my sense of compassion—having experienced what rock bottom felt like—and now had a better appreciation of what others were feeling when they were suffering.

The concept of mindfulness was new to me. I still couldn't even properly define what it was. From what I had read, mindfulness was the act of being aware of your thoughts and your feelings. In theory, that's what this whole transition had been about. Before the separation, I had never even considered thinking about my thoughts. But I had no idea if I was doing the whole *mindfulness* thing properly.

As for confidence, it had been crushed with the separation. For someone who had always been confident and certain about which direction life was heading, the breakup had been a wrecking ball on my confidence. Confidence in myself and my future was something I was going to have to work hard to re-establish.

Reading further, I come across a passage in the book by the Dalai Lama:

> *"The true mark of a meditator is that he has disciplined his mind by freeing it from negative emotions."*

I wondered how exactly one could accomplish that. How could one be free of negative emotions while sitting in their boxers, with a burned leg, alone, depressed, with seemingly no future to look forward to? How could one be free of negative emotions when the person they loved walked out the door to choose a different life? How does one stay positive with all the negative going on in the world? I kept reading:

"But apart from lofty heights of being, there's a more practi-cal potential within each one of us: a life best described as flourishing."

"Must be nice," I mumbled to myself, as I hobbled to the kitchen to stare into an empty fridge. I was not flourishing. I was the furthest thing from it. In that moment I felt physically and emotionally shattered. I was a walking, hobbling, pity-party. A flourishing life for myself was not something I could even picture in my mind. Returning to the dining room table, my stomach still empty, I continued reading and came across Reinhold Niebuhr's serenity prayer:

"God, grant me the serenity to accept things I cannot change, courage to change things I can, and the wisdom to know the difference."

I took a deep breath, clasped my hands behind my head and stared at the ceiling. I could not change that she was gone; I could not change the throbbing pain in my leg; I could not, in that instance, change the fact that I was alone. What could I change? I thought to myself. And if I found things that I could change, perhaps with how I was thinking and feeling, would I have the courage to do so?

I opened my journal and recorded the thoughts that had come up after reading the quotes. The journaling and meditation had become a daily practice since those early dark days after the breakup. Like I was doing on that day, I would often re-write compelling passages from whatever book I was reading. By writing them out by hand, it was as though my brain would slow down and be better able to comprehend the wisdom in the teaching. I had never been so driven to comprehend at a higher level. As an engineer, I needed to solve this challenge that had been thrust upon me: I had to figure out how to get a better hold of my mind so that I could move away from the painful lows that I kept feeling. I couldn't go the rest of my life having darkness within me; I had to figure this out. I had to figure me out.

I read on to one final passage in the book:

> *"Being real means being honest that you're not living the dream."*

The message landed like a ton of bricks. I had been living the dream, at least over the past three weeks of trips. But permanently living that freedom and living my dream life every day, that was a different story. I wondered if skiing every day even was my dream life. I liked it, but there must be more to life than just sliding down a hill. I had to figure out what my dream life was going to be, especially now that I had been forced to throw out the old version. I had some serious thinking to do to get clear on what I wanted.

Things started look up later in the week. My leg had finally healed enough to allow me to wear pants and leave the condo. I put in a long and productive morning at the office before heading downtown for meetings. The productivity made me feel like a contributing member of society again. I was energized by the return to work and my impending birthday the next day.

Back home that evening, I cracked open a bottle of red wine to start a pre-birthday party for one. Thinking ahead to my birthday, I sent out texts to friends with details of a last-minute gathering at my place. I wracked my brain to think of everyone I could invite. This year, more than ever, I wanted a condo full of people to celebrate with me.

I wanted great music, great conversations, a memorable party that my friends would enjoy. Above all, I wanted to feel good again. What I didn't want was a pity party.

With a second glass of wine, I thought ahead to turning thirty-seven. I gave myself a pep talk. "Mike, you've got this. You have skills, a job, a condo, money in the bank, creativity, freedom—you have so much it's scary." I thought back to my recent three weeks of travel. While it wasn't a flawless journey without its challenges, I did still enjoy the distraction and the change of scenery. With travel in mind, I made a rough plan to get through the next six months. I would soon be leaving for three months of work in Victoria, which would be a great change to get out of my familiar life in Vancouver. After that, depending on what I could negotiate with work, I could go down to Nicaragua where my sister had just purchased a property. Then on the way home I could swing back through Kingston and Toronto to see family and friends. I could even go to New York City—a place that I'd always wanted to visit. It was an ambitious plan to get me through the first half of the year. But it felt good, like something I could look forward to. To celebrate my plan, I poured another glass of wine, finishing the bottle.

Soon after, I made the very poor choice to open a second bottle. "Screw it," I said to myself—tomorrow was my birthday, I deserved to celebrate. As I listened to a playlist that I had created for my party the next night, I looked around the dark, art-filled condo and smiled at the hard, but meaningful times I'd had in this place over the past few months. I wondered what my future would be in this space. Would I ever get back to living a normal life in our former matrimonial home?

With a surge of energy, I started moving around the living room furniture to create a new layout. I hadn't used the TV for months, so I gave it a new permanent home in the closet. I had found that I had too much of my own thinking and reading to do, that I had completely lost any interest in what was on TV. It felt great to officially get rid of it and free up some new space; both in the condo, and in my mind.

With an hour to go until midnight, I was back at the dining room table in a tired haze of drunkenness. I thought ahead to potentially more travel in the fall: my cousin was getting married on the US east coast, I could surely attend. My mind drifted to my cousin's dad (my uncle), who was a brain surgeon. His brother (my dad), a judge. My mom a professor, my older sister a doctor, and my younger sister a nurse. How lucky were they to serve others in their professions?

Then I wondered again, what was I? What was this new appreciation of art I was developing? How could I make my own art? Was making art my true calling? Was I supposed to be an artist, not an engineer? And if so, an artist in what? I certainly could not draw to save my life—as exhibited through my tragic tattoo sketch. I could take great photos, but that passion had faded over the years. What about writing?

I had been journaling for a few months and had enjoyed it. The train of ideas had come easily and helped sort through the many questions in my mind. I'd shared that piece with Stacey (the radio host) and received a decent review. I wondered, could I be a writer? Could that be my original art? But what would I write about?

Digging through my mind, I arrived at what I knew best: the pain I'd been experiencing since Rebecca walked out the door. I thought back to the early days after the breakup, the restaurant-tear-tour that started with that first dinner with Jessie. In my journal I wrote about the feelings I had that night, the description of the dark restaurant, the hands held across the table, the tears we shared.

I thought about what else I could write about. I thought back again to my second dinner with Ash, on Main Street. I remembered asking if she could write about what changes were going on in my head. She was a journalist after all, so she knew how to write—a skill which I didn't think I had in me. She had politely declined. But what if it was me who wrote about it? The pain, the anger, the hurt, the sorrow, the deep moan that exited my body when I knew it was all over. I could write about it all. But why? Who would care? What would be the point? And how would it all end? Plus, if I was being honest with myself, I didn't know how to write. I must know someone else who could better tell the story. Exhausted, and with no clear answers, I headed off to bed. The one thing I did know for sure was that I'd be waking up to a pounding headache on my birthday.

I awoke with my predicted hangover early the next morning. Thoughts from the night before sloshed around in my head. I tried rolling into different positions to reduce the pain in my head so I could think clearly. I found a position lying on my side with my head propped up. With my mind somewhat clear, I returned to my thoughts about writing my story.

If I were to commit to such a project—whether I wrote it or someone else—the key would be to nail the emotions: the highs and the lows of everything that had happened. For it to work, for the story to resonate, every experience would have to be included: the breakup, the breakdown, the art, the concert, the hockey game, the circus, the ski trips, Kingston, Toronto, and New Year's Eve. I wondered if I would be comfortable sharing all of that. My next question was, how would it all end? Could I write the end of my own story before it happened in real life? My head pounded with a mix of excitement and dehydration. I limped out of bed into my running shoes with hopes of sweating out the alcohol on a run.

Halfway through the cold, misty run I started to feel better. I thought ahead to Victoria and how good it would be to have a change of scenery. In Vancouver, I wasn't eating enough, sleeping enough, exercising enough, I wanted all of that to change while I was in Victoria. On top of that, I needed a fresh new space to do some deeper thinking. I had to better understand the awareness that was growing within me. I had to learn how to channel it towards creating a new future. I had to figure out exactly what I wanted that new future to be. Above all, I had to figure out how to stop bouncing between these higher highs and lower lows. I had to pin life on high. Victoria would be my saviour, I hoped.

———————

It was sometime after two in the morning, long after the last guests had gone home. Justin held my hands across the dining room table while giant tears rolled down my face. "It's okay, man, just let it out," he said. He had come over from Victoria for my birthday party and was staying the night, crashing on the couch. We were finishing the last remnants of alcohol when I lost it and the emotions flooded out.

"I don't want to be alone," I managed to get out between sobs, "I don't know what I'm going to do. I'm trying everything I can to move on in my mind, but I always get sucked back to the pain. It's been over two months, I'm tired of feeling like hell."

Justin just listened and nodded. I felt his empathy and compassion from across the table. As painful as the moment was, it was the highlight of my night. My lofty expectations for the party were unrealistic. The night was largely disappointing. Was an event full of interesting people engaged in meaningful conversation too much to ask for on my birthday? Or perhaps, all that occurred, and I wasn't present enough to take it in. Either way, it was over, and I was glad.

"How do you do it, man? How do you handle being on your own when everyone else is coupled up?" I asked Justin.

"I don't know, I've always been good at being alone."

"I guess so. It's just so new for me. Still so sudden, after all those years being together."

"I can't even imagine. Just give it time. It will get better."

"I hope so. I'm looking forward to getting out of here soon and going to Victoria. I need a change of scenery. A new start. That will help."

"Absolutely."

"There's nothing left to drink, man, let's call it a night."

"Good call."

The next day was spent in the thick fog that follows two nights of heavy drinking. Justin left in the morning to make his way back to Victoria. I managed to pull myself out of the condo sometime late in the afternoon to head out for fast food. I felt heavy, sad, and alone. The birthday, as anticlimactic as it was, was my last distraction before truly facing the uncertain year ahead. I wasn't drinking a ton more than usual, but my head and body seemed to be rejecting the alcohol more than ever before. At the same time, I couldn't even consider getting through all those lonely nights without something to take the edge off. The alcohol would temporarily numb the pain, but it seemed to slide me down into a deeper low with each hangover. Something had to give. I couldn't go on like this.

Later that night I took my familiar perch at the dining room table for a night of introspection and writing in my journal. My first thoughts were that I didn't have to live in this space anymore, I didn't have to stay in the condo if it was contributing to my pain. But if I were to permanently leave, and do something different, would that automatically make me happy? Also, why was I still hurting so much? Was she hurting this much too?

The sadness, the weight of the emotions, the uncertainty about the future, the embarrassment of her leaving, the tightness in my chest, everything that I had largely avoided during the past few weeks of distractions, had returned with a vengeance. I must deal with this before it ruined the entire year. But how?

I remembered that earlier in the day I had seen a quote somewhere online that read: "Choose happy, time is precious." It couldn't be that simple. Was happiness just a choice that could be made? And if so, how could we change our mind? If it were that easy, wouldn't everyone do it? My thoughts swirled and landed on what had recently brought me joy: the arts, music, writing, being in nature. I must keep digging into those things; they were my way out of this darkness.

I moved to the living room to sprawl on the carpet as rain tapped the skylight above. Scrolling through social media, I came across a quote from the Buddha: "The root of all suffering is desire." What was it I was desiring? To have someone to love? How could I get rid of that desire; isn't that what all humans want? Was I desiring a certain type of birthday party? Absolutely. What if I had approached the night with no expectations and instead been present and grateful for my friends that had come? To remove all desire meant I had to learn how to be grateful for all that I had in the present moment. I had far more than many. I had my health. I had a place to call home. I had my education. I had the means to travel. I had just done two incredible ski trips that most people could only dream of. I was the definition of privileged, but still, I was suffering.

Thoroughly confused, I came across another quote on social media, this one by C. Assaad:

> *"Close your eyes and imagine the best version of you possible. That's who you really are, let go of any part of you that doesn't believe it."*

I closed my eyes as I sprawled out on the living room carpet. I couldn't see it. I couldn't see the best version of me. Who was I supposed to be? What was I capable of becoming? What did I want to become? All I could see, and feel, was a lonely, hungover, thirty-seven-year-old lying on the floor alone on a Saturday night. Surely this wasn't the best possible version of me.

Even if I could imagine a better version of me, what good would that do? How could I transform that vision into reality? My mind raced ahead to my upcoming time in Victoria, maybe things could be different there. Maybe in a new space, with new routines, I could get clearer on the best version of me. Maybe, once I had that clarity, I could learn how to step into this new me. At the very least, hopefully I could step out of this cycle of brief cresting highs followed by long troughs of lower lows. Maybe in Victoria I would find my true self.

It was time for bed. I got changed and dropped down in a heap of exhaustion. I journaled a few final thoughts for my subconscious to process before drifting off to sleep: "Be present...nourish your mind, body, soul...visualize the life that you want...travel...adventure...love... believe in it, believe in you, and it will come true."

———————

After a Sunday of exercise, meditation, and time outside, I started the work week with a renewed sense of optimism. The daily meditation, along with the journaling, had been the two most impactful things (so far) that had come into my life since the breakup. I was still doing the guided meditations through the app on my phone, but I was eager to learn new techniques.

After a turbulent first two weeks to start the year, I was ready to start over. I would go to Victoria, I would focus on work and have new experiences in a new space, I would work hard, then take time off in the spring to focus on me. The future was in my hands.

As I walked to work Monday morning, I thought more about what I wanted my future to look like. I'd always wanted to travel and work remotely—live the laptop lifestyle working from remote tropical beaches. It looked so good for others on social media. I wondered if I could make it happen for me. I also wondered if I could find a partner to complement that lifestyle. A partner that would allow me space to work a few hours each day, but also join me in adventures, listen to music, sit by a fire at night, laugh, make love.

I also wondered if I could stay in my current job and do it from other corners of the planet. Why couldn't I work a few hours each morning leaving time to explore nature and new cultures in the afternoons? Evenings could be spent with music and dancing with a gorgeous partner. Was this what I really wanted for my future? In the past, my thinking towards the future had been linear and predictable. Keep working, make more money, get a bigger place to live, do a few trips, have some kids, get old. Now I had been presented—against my will— with a blank slate to fill in however I wanted. It was at times exciting, but equally overwhelming. Plus, it was so new to be planning a future without my wife's input. We were still sporadically in touch by text, but for the most part, we were doing well at giving each other space. As for what I wanted for my future, I needed to do more thinking.

Five days later I was sampling a vision of a future that included more art. I was in Whistler for the weekend and had convinced a few of my friends to skip our usual bar night in favour of a live painting exhibit. The event was held at the Audain Art Gallery, an award-winning building with long concrete corridors complemented by soaring wood ceilings, and expansive windows looking out to the nearby forest. A DJ played music to the mountain hipster crowd as three artists completed live paintings of mountain landscapes.

After a few drinks I approached one of the artists to chat about her painting. A petite blonde woman with the arms of a rock climber, she was quick to mention her boyfriend. Was it that obvious I was now single? I hadn't worn my wedding ring since Rebecca walked out the door. Which was sad because I'd always loved wearing it. It was comforting being 'taken' and not having to worry about finding a partner. We had designed our wedding bands and her engagement ring together. My ring had the unique feature of being square on the sides to fit more comfortably. Now it sat buried in a forgotten drawer back at the condo.

I pushed on with the artist, sharing my new interest in art, showing her pictures of the prints that hung on my walls back in Vancouver. "I love them!" she said. It felt good to establish a connection with someone new. Meanwhile, my friends were already losing interest in the event and started to gather their coats. I knew this had been a stretch for them to come to the event. But they had agreed, I am sure to somewhat satisfy me. As much as the last few months had been an adjustment for me, it had also meant an adjustment for my friends and family. None of them wanted to see me in pain. They were used to seeing me happy, and together with Rebecca. On top of that, they didn't know what to think when I started to share more of my thoughts on social media. Either way, they had come with me that night, and helped me take the next steps towards a future that included more art.

The next morning, my friends headed out to ski. We had spent the night at my friend's family's townhouse near Alta Lake. I chose to skip skiing and stay behind by the woodburning fireplace. I savoured the quiet space while taking in the mountain views across the valley. Sitting with only the sound of the crackling fire, my mind drifted back to the time I had spent in Whistler following graduation from high school.

For three months, I lived the ski-bum lifestyle with two of my friends. We survived off white rice, hot dogs, and beer. My health suffered dramatically, and I was sick for a month; but it was all worth it. I was on the hill every day, either working as a lifty or skiing on my days off.

A love for Whistler was something that Rebecca and I also shared. Our mutual passion for the mountain town—two hours from Vancouver—meant that it was the obvious location for our wedding. We were married after the busy summer months, in September. By all accounts it was the perfect day. Our friends and family basked in the late summer heat as my dad acted as the officiant for the ceremony. After the sun went down the party moved inside for a night of speeches, food, and dancing. Three days later we were off to complete the fairy tale with a honeymoon in Maui.

In Maui, I spent the mornings surfing, while Rebecca stayed behind at the hotel, reading. I didn't think much of it at the time, but perhaps this was the first sign that our separate interests would lead us apart. As the years went by, I spent more and more time doing my sports, either alone or with my buddies. Rebecca and I had tried on a few occasions to ski or bike together, but it never really worked for either of us. Eventually she developed passions of her own. It was she who pointed out that I may be better off with a different partner who was more into sports. But I never saw it. I always thought that if we were content doing our own things, we could still be together in a strong partnership. My train of thought was interrupted when a log crackled in the fire. It was ironic that I had chosen to skip skiing on this day and instead opted for a day in the village, something that she would have loved.

After a morning yoga class, I made my way to the tattoo studio. It was time to do something I had thought about for years: it was time to get my first tattoo. I met the tattoo artist at the front of the small shop to go over all the details. "Are you sure that's how you spell it?" she asked, "We only get one crack at this."

"Good point let me double check," I said.

After a search online we were good to go with my two words—*satori ananda*—the two words that summed up everything I'd been experiencing over the previous months. As we made our way to the back room and the tattoo table, I was disappointed the artist didn't want to know more about the meaning of these two words. I was trusting her with permanently altering my skin with two words that were representing the most transformative time of my life, and she didn't want to know what they meant? I mean, really. But my expectations of her interest were less important than letting her do her work. I kept quiet as I sat on her table.

The tattoo hurt like hell. The five-second increments felt like being repeatedly stung by a swarm of bees. I breathed out as she applied the ink to the top of my left rib cage underneath my arm. When she took the needle away to reposition, I would breathe in. Soon I added the words she was tattooing to my cycles of breath: *satori* on the inhale, *ananda* on the exhale. I was using the words as a mantra to get me through the discomfort of the procedure. For years I had wanted a tattoo but had never been able to commit. The thought of getting something permanently drawn on my body was overwhelming. I had a few concepts that I had liked, but nothing that had been meaningful enough to follow through on.

Despite the discomfort, I felt calm as she wrote the words across my skin in cursive writing. This time in my life, the pain, the anguish, the suffering, the breakthroughs, the realizations, the highs, the lows, were like nothing I had ever experienced before. The flashes of enlightenment, my *satori* moments, were equal parts beautiful in their clarity, and painful with their hard truths. Throughout my struggle, when I had managed to be fully in the present moment, whether observing nature, or just my breath, I had felt complete bliss, *ananda*. Twenty minutes later it was done: *satori ananda*, two words, my two words, to travel with me for all of time.

Halfway through the next week I was pulled down from my high after the thrill of the weekend and my new tattoo. I seemed to be riding an endless wave of feeling at the extremes: higher highs and lower lows. Back in the dark, cold, wet city, I experienced a whole new feeling of discomfort, during a call from my doctor.

With hopes of solving the ongoing mystery of the pain in my chest, I had recently had a CT scan. The pain had been present since the middle of the previous year. The doctor had called to give me the results from the scan. During our call, he informed me that he had discovered white spots on my lungs, a potentially much larger issue than my unsolved chest pain. "The spots are most likely just calcifications, but we won't know until you meet with a lung specialist," said the doctor.

You've got to be kidding me, I thought after hanging up the phone. Why was the Universe putting me though all these challenges? Why was I being repeatedly tested? Hadn't I endured enough? I promised myself not to worry, at least not too much. I trusted my doctor, and it was probably nothing. But still, I could appreciate how others could drive themselves mad with worry. Then again, what if it *was* something more? What if it *was* cancer? Was that all there was to my life? A privileged childhood, a brief adolescence, ending with a destructive separation. Now my life potentially taken while I'm struggling to shake being at my all-time low? Surely, that couldn't be it. Surely, I would get another chance to make the most of my life.

Still, I wondered why so many challenges? The initial pain of the separation, the disruptive Christmas travel, the daily battle to prepare healthy food, the sauna incident, now the CT scan. If the Universe was testing me, how much more did I have to learn? I was learning more about myself, but it was exhausting. And what was the purpose of all this growth and self-reflection, other than to wear me down? Any rest would have to wait a little longer, my next challenge was scheduled for the following day: the hard conversation I'd been putting off with my boss.

On our way to our lunch meeting the next day I could sense my boss's nervousness. An impromptu lunch meeting was something I had never requested before. I suspected that she thought I was considering a different job elsewhere, so I put her mind at ease. "I'm not quitting, by the way," I said, as we walked towards a café near the office.

"Oh, well that's good," she said, "Then, what's up?"

"Rebecca and I separated a few months ago. Nobody in the office knows. I thought it was time to tell you."

"Oh no, I'm so sorry. That's so hard. How are you?"

"I'm doing okay, I guess. Some days are better than others. It has been good to be busy with work and other distractions. I'm looking forward to going to Victoria. That will be a good change."

After a short walk we arrived at the café. We ordered sandwiches and took a seat near the front window. Once the sandwiches arrived, I nervously shared my thoughts about possibly taking some time off following the Victoria project. Again, she was supportive. I pushed a little further with my idea of working remotely while traveling to extend my time away from the office. "I'll have to think about how that could work. That's not something we typically do," she said.

I wasn't too discouraged with her reply, I had plenty of time to show how I could be trustworthy working remotely while I was in Victoria. Though I anticipated our conversation to be much more uncomfortable, by overcoming my fear and talking honestly with her, our talk turned out to be the high point of my day.

By the end of the week, the Victoria project had been green-lighted to start. I loaded the truck with surfboards, a mountain bike, and the espresso machine, and drove to catch the ferry to Vancouver Island. I was ready for a fresh start in a new city; I was ready to leave behind the oscillations between higher highs and lower lows; I was ready to live a life of bliss.

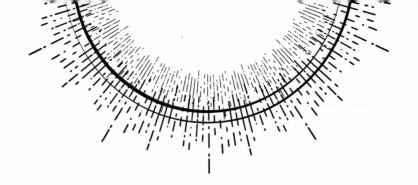

CHAPTER 7

RETURN TO DARKNESS

Only in the darkness can you see the stars.

MARTIN LUTHER KING, JR.

M y first morning in Victoria started with an online guided meditation led by one of my favourite teachers: David Ji. I was using all my tools with hopes of preventing any darkness from entering my new space. I opened the app on my phone and loaded his "Opening Your Chakras" meditation. The meditation was focused on opening the seven energy centres, or chakras, starting at the base of the spine, up to the crown of the head. The idea was to clear any emotional blockages to allow energy to flow freely and promote spiritual growth. By opening the chakras and allowing energy to flow, Ji suggested that an electromagnetic field could be created around the body. This field could be used to attract all the positive things one desired to manifest. I was still relatively new to meditation, and I couldn't prove all the spiritual promises, but I could not argue with the fact that I felt calm and peaceful during meditation, as well as afterwards—and that was something that I was desperately trying to consistently achieve in my world.

After the meditation ended, I slowly opened my eyes and took in my new surroundings. For the first portion of my time in Victoria, I had rented a loft apartment in a historic corner of downtown. The main features of the loft were twin eight-foot windows set against a sixteen-foot tall brick wall. Stairs led up to a second floor sleeping loft and vintage stereo system. The main floor had another bedroom and a modern open-concept kitchen and living room. The entire space was professionally designed with plants and a mix of antique and modern furniture. The owner, who was obviously a spiritual person, had several crystals spread throughout the loft. I wasn't familiar with the power of crystals, but I did know they were supposed to bring positive healing energy. The tall ceilings, the open space, and the healing crystals were just the change I thought I was looking for.

I spent the rest of the morning unpacking. A few hours in, I took a break on the white couch in front of the tall windows. Lying down with my feet up on the far arm rest, I picked up Rupi Kaur's *Milk and Honey*[4], the same book of poetry I had ridiculed at Christmas. A day earlier, when I was packing in Vancouver, I decided at the last minute to bring the book, along with Kaur's other piece of work, *The Sun and Her Flowers*[5].

I put the book down partway through reading the chapter on healing. Kaur was speaking directly to my wounded soul. Tears formed in

---

4 Kaur, Rupi. *Milk & Honey*. Andrews McMeel Publishing, 2015.

5 Kaur, Rupi. *The Sun and Her Flowers*. Simon & Schuster, 2017.

my eyes as she described the unraveling of her identity after experiencing a traumatic breakup of her own. Her words were raw, vulnerable, and honest. She was able to transfer her emotions and feelings into concise poems. Her words landed in the cracks that had formed in my heart. We were momentarily connected by our pain. She held nothing back, sharing her darkest moments of heartbreak, physical abuse, and rape. Kaur was healing herself by stripping away all the veils and sharing her hurt. It was as though, by sharing her darkest moments, she was giving me permission to do the same. I read a few more of her poems before drifting off into a nap. As I closed my eyes, I dreamt of being able to write with a similar grace.

As my first week in Victoria progressed, I came to the realization that the change of scenery was not going to be my saviour. Even though I was living in a new city, a new space, seeing new places, one thing remained the same: I was still with me. I was still inside the same troubled head that had burdened me back in Vancouver. I should have learned this lesson after my previous short trip to Victoria before Christmas. But I was stubborn; and it often took multiple teachings of the same message before I absorbed life's lessons.

During the first week I went out for drinks with Justin, only to be uninspired by the lack of depth in our conversation. I met another group of friends for drinks, only to focus on the fact that I was the only one who wasn't married with children. I went to a new kick-boxing studio and judged all the ways it was inferior to my gym back in Vancouver. I was stuck in a new low, but this time, in a new city. If my time in Victoria was going to help me change, that change was not going to come solely from new surroundings. With three months to endure, I had to get clear about how I wanted to intentionally spend my time.

At the end of the first week, I spent Friday night alone in the loft.

Sitting on the sofa in front of the tall windows, I made a list of how I wanted my time in Victoria to unfold. First and foremost, I had to get back to feeling healthy again. I knew I always felt better when I was exercising and eating well. I would make exercise a priority: I would bike, run, and surf. I would make a better effort at keeping the fridge full of healthy food.

Secondly, I needed to maintain a clearer mind so I could focus more purposefully on the changes going on inside of me. I would continue to meditate daily, and I would also find a yoga studio where I could practice. I would also try to drink less. This simple thought was a major revelation for me. I had been drinking more since the separation to help escape my racing mind, but the hangovers were holding me back from further growth. It presented an easy escape when negative thoughts were present, but the drinking was doing more harm than good.

I would continue to read and write and explore learning more about the 'awareness muscle' I was building. I would continue to focus on staying present, because I knew that keeping my attention on the present moment was where I found the most peace. If I could stay on track and stay focused, all the items on my list would help me create the environment to learn more about who I was. The reality was that it was easy to make plans, but without someone or something holding me accountable, it would be a challenge to implement those plans.

Despite my best intentions, I couldn't shake the darkness that followed me to Victoria. Into my second week I wondered how people lived in such a prolonged funk. I felt for them. More than ever before I could relate to how it felt to have little hope. Regardless of how much I meditated, or what books I read, I couldn't shake the sorrow of having lost her. The realizations and breakthroughs, as well as the stimulation that accompanied them, had started to wane in recent weeks. In their place came a return to the normalcy of daily routine. A void had been left in the space within me that used to house our love. The hopes and dreams had been sucked out of this space and replaced with a heavy shadow. The depths of this blackness would be triggered whenever I heard sad music. The lyrics would transport me back to our time together, and tears would take over. I cried every day of those first two weeks in Victoria.

Towards the end of my second week I made plans to meet my brother-in-law for drinks. "Are you coming over, bud?" he texted, from across the street at the Drake. He was there already, finishing drinks with one of his friends. But on that day, like many others, I just couldn't bring myself to do it. I couldn't manage to pick myself up off the couch and walk across the street. I just, couldn't. "Sorry, dude, I can't make it. I'm just not feeling it," I replied.

"Totally cool, man. No worries at all," he texted.

He knew I was hurting. How could I not be? It had still only been a few months. Even though he and Rebecca had never really got along, he knew I needed more time to heal. I wondered if maybe he knew all along our relationship wouldn't go the distance.

Sitting alone in the loft on Saturday morning, I received a text from my buddy, Bryson. "You want to go for a ride, bru?"

"Heck ya I do. Thanks for reaching out," I replied.

Bryson was an engineering classmate from university. I'd always looked up to him and jumped at the chance to share a few hours of mountain biking. With a beautiful wife, two kids, and surfing skills I could only dream of, the South African transplant had always excelled at living his life to its fullest. A few years back he took three years off to sail around the globe, chasing the world's best surf breaks while bringing awareness to the rising levels of plastic in our oceans.

I packed up my gear and made the short drive out of town to meet him. Halfway through our ride we paused to take in the view after a strenuous climb. "So how you been doing, bru?" Bryson asked, as we caught our breath standing amongst the arbutus trees.

"Well, it feels good to be outside, to be riding again. But otherwise it's been super tough. The fall sucked, obviously, then I did a bunch of travel to be distracted. I was naively hoping that when I moved over to Victoria a couple of weeks ago that everything would magically fix itself—that I would feel better. Turns out that's not exactly how it works," I said.

"Ah, that sucks, man, sorry to hear."

"Truly does, but it is what it is."

"It'll get better bru, time will heal. It always does."

"I sure hope so, because I can't go on like this forever."

"You'll be good. There must be something going around right now though, two of my other buddies just split up, one of them has kids too. It's super sad."

"Oh, no way, man, I can't imagine how hard that must be."

"Me neither," he said.

"It seems like so many people are waking up in their thirties realizing that they, or their spouse, just aren't who they thought they were."

"Ya, man. Too true. Me and the wife used this as our wake-up call, to really check in with each other and make sure we are still on the same page."

"Well at least something good has come out of all these messes. Anyways, on with it—let's ride."

"Sounds good."

After our ride I headed back downtown to the loft before showering and driving out to my sister's for dinner. The bike ride in the fresh air had helped my sour mood. I was beginning to generate some optimism that I could once and for all dig myself out of my damn hole. Arriving at my sister Jenn's place, I greeted her and Scott before heading to the living room to hang with my nieces. Not long after, we gathered around the dining room table for dinner. Sitting in between my nieces, I looked over at their family chalkboard on the far wall of the living room. On it, my oldest niece had been practicing her handwriting and had written out a list of her favourite people: Mom, Dad, Maddy (her sister), Mike and Rebecca (my ex).

That stung. Just when I had started to feel better after a day of biking, this innocent oversight had derailed me. Again, I was bounced between feeling better and sinking back down into the hurt. I wondered why I was still so fragile. Why wasn't I strong enough not to let something like this affect me? What was I doing wrong? On my own, I wasn't mentally strong enough to avoid letting my emotions derail me. The list was obviously missed by my sister, but it still hurt. The next pain I felt was when I realized that someone was going to have to explain to these two sweet girls why the aunt, whom they loved so much, was no longer going to be a part of their lives.

I was riding a low when the next week started. I was tired of feeling like shit. I needed some help to put the past behind me and start focusing on the future. It had been almost four months since she left. I had grieved and cried more than ever before in my life. I had reflected on what had gone wrong, and what I could have done better. I had acknowledged the parts of my personality that I wanted to work on. I had read book after book to better understand the realizations I had experienced. I had removed television and all the negative news to create space for more positivity. Yet, I was still struggling.

During a break at work on Monday, my third week in Victoria, I sent a text to my friend Jake, who had endured a hard breakup of his own. "Dude, any advice?"

"Yes. Keep your head up. Make plans. Be with family and friends. Be good to yourself. Distractions are good. Exercise, and let time pass," he said.

I thought about his text all day. I had been doing most of those things, but still I could do better.

The work week had gotten off to a slow start but eventually started moving well. The type of work I was doing on the construction site was both a blessing and a curse. The project involved using dredging equipment to remove contaminated sediments from the seafloor, barge the sediments to disposal facilities, then fill in the dredged areas with clean material to restore the area closer to its original healthy ecosystem. Each day I got picked up dockside and boated the short ride to the dredging barge. As the on-site engineer, my job was to keep track of construction progress on behalf of the client. Most importantly, my role was to identify any issues before they escalated and impacted the project budget or schedule.

As an engineer on a barge full of contractors, I was the odd man out. Despite the mutual goal to complete the project on time and on budget, it was an interesting dynamic, being embedded in the contractor's territory. The unspoken agreement said that if the work got done as per the design, then I had no intention of intervening and making the contractor's life difficult. The first couple of weeks were spent feeling each other out, trying to gauge how we worked together. My main role was to watch the work as it happened. On a dredging project, it was the equivalent of watching paint dry. In between repositioning the barge and dealing with frequent breakdowns, there was a lot of down-time. Herein lay my challenge: how to occupy my mind on-site when things were moving slowly.

My hope was that it would do my head some good being out of the office and on-site. What I didn't consider was that I would have even more time to let my mind wander. In my current state, that was not a good thing. It was going to be a long three months unless I could learn how to better manage my thoughts. After that, my next challenge would be to find the best use of the downtime while trapped on the barge.

Towards the end of the third week I had to head back to Vancouver for my appointment with the lung specialist. Over the previous weeks I had managed to avoid excessive worry about whatever he was going to say. It was out of my control. Still, in the back of my mind existed the possibility that he could deliver some bad news about the unknown white spots on my lungs.

To get to Vancouver, I took an early morning float plane out of Victoria harbour. After landing in Vancouver, I called a taxi to get across town to the doctor's office. It was a short wait before I was called into see the doctor. The doctor, an older man with a greying beard, gave a brief review of the tests that were run. Then he shared the re-sults: everything came back negative. As expected, the spots on my lungs were harmless calcifications from a past illness. I had a moment of elation followed quickly by more questions. I was healthy, but the original problem, my ongoing chest-pains, remained a mystery. "So, what about the pain that has been in my chest for the past six months, doctor?" I asked.

"Well, based on all the tests and procedures that you've had, you are perfectly healthy. Anything else been going on in your world?" asked the doctor.

"Um, well, ya. My marriage ended," I said.

"Sorry to hear, but that could be your answer."

"No way," I said.

"The stress, the shallow breathing, the uncertainty, a troubled mind; it can all contribute to create pain in the physical body."

"Wow, I had no idea the body could respond like that."

"Oh ya, the body hears what the mind thinks. The body is far more intelligent than we give it credit for."

"You know what it was this whole time, doctor?"

"What's that?"

"It was my heart breaking."

"So sorry, my man. At least you now have some clarity."

I left the doctor's office relieved. I wasn't sick from an illness. At the same time, I was reminded just how hard that last six months had been. The pain in my chest had started months before the breakup. Did my body know what was happening before the breakup occurred? Was the tightening in my chest a response to the change in her energy? I wondered, if I had been more in tune with my body, could I have been more aware of how seriously things were escalating before it was too late? It didn't matter, there was nothing I could do now. I was grateful for my health, but I was also more aware than ever of how much she had meant to me, and how much it hurt to lose her.

My engineering office was a short walk away from the doctor's. I stopped by to say hello to some colleagues and catch up on paperwork. After a few hours, I called for a taxi to take me back downtown to the float plane terminal for the return flight to Victoria. As I waited in the terminal for the flight to be called, I paused to reflect on what I had learned. With the clean bill of health, the weight that I had been carrying had been lifted. I felt as though I was not only shedding the uncertainty about the pain I had carried, but also the connection to my former life. I was getting closer to letting go of the chord that had connected us. This was an equally painful and freeing realization.

The float plane ride between Vancouver and Victoria was only thirty-five minutes. I spent the short flight gazing out the window, lost in thought. I was inching closer to letting go of her. The thought was painful; we had shared so many good memories together. Memories that I had trained myself not to think about over the past few months. It was just too hard. I had become very aware when my mind started to relive the past. Whenever it happened, I would tell my mind, "NO", and redirect my focus. It hadn't worked every time, but it had helped me become more aware of my thoughts. Especially the ones that no longer served me.

Halfway through the flight the small sixteen-seat float plane crossed over the Southern Gulf Islands. The scenery was like no other place on earth. The clouds that had been present throughout the day began to lift. The mid-afternoon sun touched the tiny islands below. The islands were covered with a lush, green west coast forest. They were radiant in the glow of the sun, after a long winter of damp rain. The shallow inlets along the rocky shores glowed turquoise where the light penetrated the ocean waters. I had been fortunate to fly the route several times, and each flight took my breath away. Thoughts of the chest pain, the breakup, my uncertain future, all of it, faded away. I felt light, I felt free. I wondered how long the feeling would last.

I was still feeling good through the weekend. Monday was a holiday, so two friends, Andrew and Brad, came over to visit from Vancouver. The plan was to go out on the town Sunday night, then head to the coast on Monday for some surfing. Sunday night we headed out for drinks at Saint Franks. We entered the dark, narrow, pulsing lounge, and were lucky to find the last three seats at the bar. The place was packed with people taking advantage of the long weekend. The energy was great and was fueled by a DJ playing Nineties hip hop. I recognized the bartender as a barista from a local coffee shop. Once the connection was made, the drinks started flowing.

Two beers in I started a conversation with an army veteran sitting beside me. At first, I was drawn in by the quality of our conversation, but soon it became obvious that his time served had left him with a serious case of post-traumatic stress disorder. I felt so badly for him, especially considering that he joined the army to serve others. I wanted to help him, but all I could do in that moment was listen to his stories. He ordered another drink and his voice grew louder. I knew even if I could help, it was not the time nor the place.

I excused myself and we shook hands. "You're a good man," he said, looking deep into my eyes. I felt his sincerity. I wondered if I had helped him just by listening, by seeing him, by letting him tell his stories. Maybe that connection had made a difference for him.

After four or five drinks, I could already feel the early stages of a hangover developing. Despite the hangovers getting worse as I got older, and my previously set intentions, I still couldn't commit to drinking less. Or not at all. Going out for drinks had been a part of my life for so long, I couldn't even fathom the thought of a life without alcohol.

Andrew left sometime around midnight, while Brad and I pushed on until closing. "Shall we head for a nightcap?" Brad asked when we eventually left Saint Franks.

"Ah, man, do you really think we need another?" I asked.

"Come on, it's a long weekend. What's still open?"

"Ugh, the only place open is my nemesis, The Drake."

"Why don't you like that place? It's totally fine."

"It's too bright. The sound system sucks. It's a crappy university bar. I've never had any fun there."

"Well, too bad, if it's the only place open, it's going to have to do."

"Ugh. Fine," I mumbled, as we started the short walk to our last drinks of the night.

My next memory was from the following morning. "Oh my god. My head. What happened?" I asked Brad, who had stayed over at the loft.

"Well, what's the last thing you remember?" Brad asked.

"I remember leaving Saint Franks. We didn't keep going after that, did we?"

"You know it. We went to The Drake."

"But I hate The Drake."

"So you mentioned. I even think you told that to our server once we got there."

"Oh, man. That's brutal. Then what happened?"

"After a couple of drinks, we stumbled back here to the loft, and you proceeded to fill the toilet with puke."

"You've got to be kidding me."

"No sir." Brad said.

"Brutal. You know I just turned thirty-seven. This is embarrassing. I'm too old for this crap."

"Ah, come on, dude, don't be so hard on yourself, we had fun."

"I'm not having fun now, and today is going to suck. Speaking of which, what time did we say we'd pick up Andrew?"

"In about ten minutes, we better hustle."

"Ugh, fine."

Brad and I gathered our surf gear and loaded up my truck. We made the ten-minute drive to pick up Andrew, who was also in rough shape. We made a stop for coffee then started the hour-and-a-half drive out to the coast. Soon after arriving at the beach, we were in the water paddling out to catch some waves. Usually the cold saltwater could cure any hangover, but not on that day. I had to start drinking less. I was still relying on the alcohol to escape the pain that lingered in my darkened soul. It was an easy out, but the aftermath meant days like this—potentially beautiful days in the ocean—were ruined. Something had to give. Soon.

The next work week passed uneventfully. It rolled by with a busy pace of long days and quiet nights. Friday night arrived, and I found myself feeling sad and alone in the loft. After the moment of bliss on the float plane a week earlier, I had progressively slipped back down into a new low. It was as though my emotions were rising and falling just like the waves I had surfed, or tried to surf, earlier in the week. The highs, the lows, the ups, the downs, the peaks, and troughs, it was exhausting. I was tired of it. I was tired of the lows. I was tired of feeling sad. I was tired of feeling hopeless. To complicate things, I had experienced those brief moments, those *satori* moments of clarity and bliss. I knew what it felt like to feel good, but I couldn't hold on to it. Like a wave, it would roll away underneath me, and I'd slide back down into a dark trough. I desperately wanted to stay on top of the wave.

Laying on the couch under the eight-foot windows, I put on some music, lit some candles, and accepted that that Friday night, like so many others, would be spent alone. I poured a glass of red wine and picked up the latest book I was reading, *Scar Tissue*[6], by the Red Hot Chili Peppers' lead singer, Anthony Kiedis. The book was a memoir about his journey to become the lead singer of one of the top bands in the world. The story of his success was remarkable considering his battle with serious drug and alcohol addictions. His writing was raw and vulnerable; he held nothing back when describing the dark places he had visited when high on drugs. The parties, the sex, the begging for drugs under highway overpasses in Los Angeles... he shared it all.

The success and fame sounded incredible, but the extreme lows that he had to endure, those I did not envy. It was powerful to be able to experience them through his words, and not have to live them myself. I was also drawn to the book because his writing style was relatively simple, certainly not overly academic. It was reassuring to see that his style could be so effective. It reminded me of my own. It had been several weeks since I had thought about writing my story, but the thought was still there.

———————

The month of March started with a visit from my mom, my younger sister Jane, her partner Travis, and their baby. It had been two months since I had seen them at Christmas in Kingston. On the first day of March, a Thursday, I started the drive out to Jenn's place where everyone was staying. I was looking forward to seeing everyone, but I was also drained after a long week of work. On top of that, I was still

6   Kiedis, Anthony. *Scar Tissue*. Hachette Books, 2005.

struggling to find consistency with my emotions. I wondered if they expected me to be back to my old self. At the same time, I wondered if I was ever going back to my old self, or if I even wanted that. As I made the drive, I reflected on just how many tears I had shed since I had last seen my mother. The thought made me shudder; surely with her motherly instincts she would be able to tell. I didn't want to disappoint her or any of my family, but I was trying my hardest to move forward, unsuccessfully.

I arrived soon after at Jenn's. I parked the truck and made my way to the front door. Once inside, I was greeted by my younger sister, Jane, who was carrying her baby boy. "The little dude has grown so much!" I said to her.

"Ya, he's a handful. The kid won't sit still," she said.

"Hi sweetie. How are you?" asked Mom, giving me a big hug.

"I'm fine, Mother. Still breathing," I said.

"Oh Michael. Here, come eat something. You look hungry, and tired," Mom said.

We all gathered around the island in Jenn's kitchen, while Scott prepared dinner. It was good to be together again. I took a brief turn holding Jane's squirming baby and managed to get a quick inhale on the top of his cute little head.

"Brother, have you gone to my favourite restaurant yet, Be Love?" asked Jenn.

"Um no. I want to, it sounds great. But I'm not too keen on going alone," I said.

"Just sit at the bar," said Jenn.

The comment stung. Jane let out a small gasp as the words came out of Jenn's mouth. Jenn meant nothing by the comment, but in my fragile emotional state, it didn't land well. I had been going to restaurants by myself for months, ever since that first journey into Barney's back in November. But for some reason, to have my aloneness broadcast in front of my family, caught me off guard. I couldn't help thinking how unfair it was that I was destined to dine alone, with my shrinking company of one, while my siblings had expanding families of their own. I wondered what the hell I had done wrong to end up like this. There was no reason for such an innocent comment to throw me off. I hoped my new level of sensitivity wasn't destined to be with me forever.

Scott continued to prepare the meal, while sneaking the odd hug with Jenn. Their kids danced in circles around the kitchen, excited to have other family members to entertain. Jane and Travis enjoyed a brief break as Mom took the baby off their hands. I sat alone with my sorrow. It wasn't as much the pain that I was frustrated with, but more the fact that I was still carrying it after all these months. I had been trying everything to shake it off, to get rid of the uninvited companion that had burrowed itself into my world. I was doing all the meditation, all the journaling, all the damn positive affirmations. Yet still, the darkness lingered. Worse, I was running out of ways to rid it from my soul.

After dinner I made a quick move to gather my things and leave. "You're leaving already?" asked Mom.

"Ya, Mom, I'm drained, and I have to work tomorrow. I'll see you guys again tomorrow night," I said.

"Alright sweetie, if you say so."

I was getting desperate. On the drive back into town I wracked my brain for what else I could do to move on, to get my life back, to reclaim the confidence I used to have. I needed to get back to a place where family dinners weren't ruined by my brittle emotions. I needed more help, to once and for all leave the darkness behind.

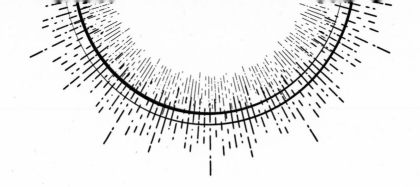

CHAPTER 8

INTO THE LIGHT

The secret of change is to focus all of your energy,
not on fighting the old, but on building the new.

DAN MILLMAN

Everything changed when Brittany entered my world. A beauty queen and former reality television star, she had recently become a life coach. I had been following her online for months. I was obviously attracted to her looks, but it was the confidence she portrayed through her posts that I was drawn to. She shared all her personal struggles through the captions that went along with her stunning photos. She motivated her followers by sharing how she overcame her battles to become a master of mental discipline. Through her coaching, she helped her clients grow this same 'discipline muscle'. That was exactly what I had been searching for to help me return into the light.

After a series of messages, we decided to connect by phone, to discuss her becoming my coach. I saw the warning signs immediately. I was considering this for all the wrong reasons because I was attracted to her. This could only lead to further hurt. I had to convince myself that it wasn't just her beauty that I resonated with. The confident way that she moved and spoke on her videos was what I needed to reclaim for myself.

Friday afternoon we had our first call during a pause in construction on-site. I was grateful that the timing of our call had corresponded with a break from the loud machinery.

"Hello Michael! How are you?" she said, to start our call.

"Oh hi, I am, um good. Thank you," I stammered.

"First up, do you prefer Mike or Michael?" she asked.

"Mike is fine."

"Okay, sounds good. So, tell me, why are you considering hiring a coach?"

"I guess well, I don't know, I'm kind of looking to move on."

"Move on from what exactly?"

I was already feeling uncomfortable. It had been some time since I had really talked about the separation, and those conversations were with close friends, not strangers. "Um, well, I separated from my wife, about four months ago. It's been, it's been hard," I said.

"I am so sorry. That must be so challenging. What do you want to move on to? What is your ideal outcome with coaching?"

"I guess I just want to feel good again, to be moving forward."

"Move forward towards what?"

"Well that's the thing, I have no idea. I've been up and down the last little while. I just can't seem to generate the mental discipline to move forward."

"Mental discipline is E-V-E-R-Y-T-H-I-N-G," she said, as she emphasized every letter in the word. "Once you master your mental discipline, your mind, you become unstoppable. Do you want to become unstoppable?"

"Um, ya, I guess so."

"You guess so?"

"I mean, yes, yes I do."

"That's more like it. What are your ten-year goals?"

"I, um, I don't have any."

"You don't have any? How can you expect to get anywhere if you don't have a destination in mind?"

"Well, I don't know. I've just been so focused on the day to day, on getting happy again."

"I see. Well what do you want your life to feel like in ten years?"

"Well, I don't know. I'll have to think about it."

"That may be one of your challenges, you think too much. You're an engineer, right?"

"Yes."

"Then it's your job to think. But sometimes you need to think less and feel more. That is your homework; to give some consideration to how you want your life to feel in ten years' time. What do you want your future to feel like? I want you to break it down into six categories: health, relationships, career, contribution, money & abundance, and mindset & consciousness. Is that clear?"

"Ya, I got it," I said, as I feverishly took down notes in the small waterproof notebook I carried on-site.

Our call was only twenty minutes, but I already felt encouraged. I was already getting a brief glimpse of what it would take for my mind to think differently, to start looking forward with a new perspective.

She was already challenging my way of thinking, or over-thinking. I could feel a small glimmer of hope that I was finally on the cusp of moving forward. I had someone in my court to support me and hold me accountable. I had found my coach.

The next day my family came downtown to meet me for lunch. After lunch, my sisters joined me on a walk to Government Street, while the others headed back out to Jenn's. After months of messaging with the thought of a sibling tattoo day, I had recently made it real by booking appointments for all three of us.

The three of us, plus Travis and the baby, squeezed into the studio's small waiting area. The walls and ceiling were lined with colourful sketches of past tattoos. I took it in and sensed the familiar pre-ink nervous energy building between the three of us. The tattoo artist came out to greet us. I tried to get a read on this stranger who was about to permanently alter our bodies. He seemed kind and had friendly eyes. We were in good hands. "Alright, who's first?" he asked. "I'll go," Jenn said, volunteering right away. She was embodying the go-first mentality she'd been teaching her kids.

Jenn got a small lotus flower on the inside of her wrist. She came out beaming with a post-ink buzz. It was a second tattoo for Jenn. Her first, just under her left shoulder blade, was a beautiful stem and flower with the words: *Grace Too*, a tribute to one of the songs by our shared hero, Gord Downie.

Reluctantly, Jane went in next. It was her third time getting a tattoo, but she was still unsure with her design of the letters: RS (her baby's initials) destined for the inside of her left wrist. Ten minutes later it was too late. She now had a symbolic reminder of her first born, to join the place he already occupied in her heart.

Finally, it was time for me to head in. I made my way into the back room and lay down on the artist's table. Thinking back over the previous months, I wanted to capture something that reflected both the highs and lows I'd been experiencing. When I was creating the design, I thought back further to the end of that first appointment with the counselor, back in November. I recalled he'd recommended that I, "Just ride the waves of emotion." At the time, I had no clue what he was talking about. Now, after living for months with the rolling wave of emotions, I had learned to appreciate what he was saying. He was suggesting that instead of trying desperately to hang on to the highs, a better approach was to be fully present and enjoy the brief moments of bliss. Just like a rolling wave, you could only sit on the peak for an instant before it rolled away underneath you. It was the same with the lows. Instead of fighting to escape being in the trough of a wave, he suggested witnessing the experience and trying to learn what lessons accompanied the tough times. We learn the most from our struggles, but rarely held that appreciation when in the dark trough between two peaks.

Twenty minutes later it was done. Getting up off the table, I looked down at the new piece of art running the length of the inside of my right forearm. It was a simple, solitary line: the crests and troughs of three waves. I loved it. Three waves to remind me of this important time in my life. Three waves to remined me to be present and be grateful for the fleeting moments of bliss. Three waves to remind me that the lows were not permanent, that they too would eventually pass. Three waves to remind me to learn from the lessons that accompanied the lows. Three waves to remind me that when the lows were just too much, when life seemed like a wild, raging storm, a wicked tempest of spray and foam blowing across the surface, I could always dive down to the calm serenity that existed in the world beneath the waves.

———————

On Mondays, work on-site didn't begin until midmorning. The start time was a few hours later than the other days of the week. I savoured the slow starts each week by doing yoga or meditation in the loft. On the Monday following the tattoos, I chose an online meditation about dharma, by David Ji. I took a comfortable seat on the couch, as I loaded the guided meditation on my phone. As with most meditations, this one started by calming the mind by focusing on the breath. Ji then gave some background on the law of dharma, which states that every single person has a purpose in life, a special talent, or a unique gift to share and teach to others. In seeking our purpose or dharma, we are seeking the pillar that will uphold everything in our existence. This is the foundation from which everything, including ourselves, will grow. When this purpose is combined with a service to others, we experience a true state of ecstasy. Reaching for my journal after the meditation, I got right to work. I must find my purpose.

Thinking back to David's words, I started to think through the guiding questions he asked: what did I love to do? What was I passionate about? What was it that, while I was doing it, time seemed to stand still? What was I doing the last time I felt joyful, deeply fulfilled, and in the zone? What were my unique abilities and distinctive talents? What did I do better than anyone else? How could I help others by using what I was good at? I was about to start answering the questions when I realized what time it was. I had to get to the job site—finding my purpose in life would have to wait.

Little was accomplished on-site that day by the contractor. A series of minor breakdowns on the barge-mounted excavator, meant that the hole that we were digging barely grew. The success of our days was measured by how much the hole grew with each shift. Since the hole was underwater, the progress was measured by a bathymetric survey that scanned the ocean floor. On paper, it was a simple job: dig a hole to remove the contaminated material, then fill the hole back in with clean material. But the simplicity of the hole dig was made more complex since we were on the ocean. Equipment failures, weather delays, environmental restrictions, all contributed to days when our progress was limited. On those days we were all frustrated. For me, on days like that, I couldn't help thinking how I could be better spending my time doing something else. Especially considering I still had so much to organize in my mind.

Back at the loft after work I slumped down on the couch. I filled the last pages of my journal with my thoughts on the slow day. I remembered I had an empty journal in the bedroom, so I got up off the couch to go search for it. It didn't take long to find it among the stack of books I had brought over from Vancouver. The journal was light brown and had a drawing of a First Nation's raven and eagle on the cover. My dad had bought it for me when we were all in Tofino six months earlier, only weeks before the breakup.

On that trip, Dad had rented two cabins at Middle Beach Lodge, for an extended long weekend. He and Monica were in one, while Jenn and her family plus Rebecca and I, shared the other. We had been to the lodge several times. It had just the right balance of west coast charm without being overly rustic.

Looking back, Rebecca had been distant the whole trip. She chose to spend the days reading alone in the main lodge, while I spent time in the ocean surfing. When I was floating alone in the ocean, I could sense that her thoughts were not with me. At that time, she had been drifting away for several months. She didn't end up staying the whole trip at the lodge. She had to get back to Vancouver for work.

On the day that she flew out of the tiny Tofino airport, we sat in silence in the small boarding area. I didn't know how to connect with her. As limited as I was in my abilities to communicate, she wasn't much better. She had been a people pleaser her whole life. I had been short-tempered and quick to anger. The combination meant that she never spoke up when something was bothering her, because I didn't know how to hear her without becoming angry and defensive. We had barely slept together over the previous months. The last time, on Labour Day, she couldn't even look at me. Afterwards, I felt disgusting, like I had violated a stranger, instead of making love to my wife. Still, I tried to bridge the gap that was lengthening between us.

"Don't worry, it'll pass. It's just a phase," she said, as we sat waiting for her plane to be called. At the time I had no idea how serious it was. I don't know if she did either. A few short weeks after that trip to Tofino she had moved out.

I took the journal with me back to the couch. I traced my hand over the red raven and eagle on the cover. On the inside of the journal the symbolism of the animals was explained. The raven was a transformer and a creator; it symbolized knowledge and wisdom. The eagle was known for its power and prestige, but also represented peace and friendship. Transformer, creator, knowledge, wisdom, power, prestige, peace, friendship—these were powerful words. I closed my eyes and meditated on these words as they rolled through my mind. My thoughts were interrupted only a minute later when my phone buzzed with a text—it was Rebecca, she wanted to talk. I wondered if it was a coincidence that she reached out only moments after I had been thinking about her? I wondered if I had made that happen.

We hadn't seen each other since the dinner on Main Street, way back in November. I had been terribly lonely without her; it was such a harsh transition to wake up one day and not have her by my side. At the same time, I hadn't really found it hard not to see her for all these months. I had so much thinking to do, and I had to do this work alone, in silence. After all, it was she who had chosen this fate for us. It was she who had walked out on our partnership.

I dialed her number as I sat on the couch. "Hi," she said, in a high-pitched surprised voice. It was surprising, to be talking again after all this time. We had kept in touch by the occasional text message, but it wasn't the best way to communicate. It was impossible to interpret tone over text. But at the same time, I didn't think there had been much to talk about: she was figuring out what she ultimately wanted, while I was also working on myself. But we both knew we couldn't go on like this forever, we had to talk at some point.

She gave a brief update about what she had been up to. Sharing enough to let me know that she was okay, but not sharing too much that it hurt me even more. I sensed that she was also still trying to figure herself out. I could feel the pain in her voice, a reflection of how much pain she had caused me. She was trying to figure out who she was, what life she wanted. It was not easy for either of us. She had been inching closer to the realization that the life that we had been living, the life that she had been living, wasn't her dream life.

I didn't share much about what I had been doing. It wouldn't have helped either of us to share details about the months I had spent crying in the streets. I did share that I would be back in Vancouver the following weekend. We agreed that it was time to meet again in person. We had to discuss next steps. She said we needed to lay *ground rules* for the separation. I didn't want to know what that meant, but agreed we had to get a better understanding about where we stood. A part of me still had a glimmer of hope for a reconciliation. I didn't know if it was possible: either if she wanted it, or if I could go down that road. What I did know was that I had changed, and I was still changing. I knew she had been shifting too. As awkward as it was going to be to meet in person, I felt peaceful knowing that it was going to be obvious if the new evolving versions of us had any hope of being compatible again.

We talked for almost an hour. It was good to communicate by phone. Laying on the couch after the call I felt free and calm. It hurt me to know that she was still hurting. She had cried several times during the call. "I will always love you. You may not believe that, or understand that, but I will always love you," she had said. I believed her, I understood her. I thought ahead to seeing her again in person. I wasn't nervous, I felt a sense of calm. I was going to be okay with either outcome: together or apart. If by some miracle she wanted to give us a try again, and if my heart was willing to consider letting her back in, then we would try that. If she didn't or I couldn't, that would be okay too. I sensed it was going to be apparent which path to take. My heart would guide me; I was beginning to learn how to trust it.

Productivity on-site improved throughout the week, as did my spirits. I was doing better controlling my erratic emotions. Friday morning came around and I lingered in bed wondering how I had arrived at such peace. Was it the sense of calm I felt after the call with Rebecca? Was it the hope, energy and optimism that had been brought into my world after my first call with Brittany? Was it the metaphors interwoven within my new wave tattoo? I wasn't sure.

I thought back to the first tattoo I had gotten two months earlier in Whistler. Since that time, whenever friends inquired about the tattoo, I had to carefully explain the meaning and the origins of the two words, *satori ananda*. I still loved my words, but it felt somewhat inauthentic to be reciting the definitions of two mutually exclusive words: I needed my own, simplified meaning for the combination of these two special words. A phrase that reflected this new state I was working towards. I lay in bed a few moments longer, staring up at the ceiling overhead. The loft, with its crystals and high ceilings, had been the perfect space to continue my evolution, my awakening. I thought back to my original intention after the separation, of one day, just being happy again. It seemed like I was finally making progress. In a moment of clarity, I received a download from above of how my two words, *satori ananda*, reflected what was transpiring on my journey. My two words defined how I had started to awaken to happiness.

On the weekend I headed back to Vancouver and up to Whistler to ski with friends. Halfway through Saturday morning we were standing on the first peak outside of the main ski area, about to begin a day of backcountry touring. The sun was out, and a fresh canvas of untracked snow covered the mountains. It was glorious. I returned yet again to my New Year's resolution to be present. It was my mantra for the day. I wanted to fully immerse myself in nature, I wanted to feel each ray of sun, I wanted to connect and laugh with my friends. I lingered behind for a few minutes taking pictures, as my friends started the first descent towards the next mountain over.

A couple of hours and a few summits later, we were standing near the base of one of the most prominent peaks in the area, Fissile Mountain. We all watched in wonder as a pair of skiers fearlessly descended a steep fifty-five degree run, through a narrow chute down the majestic mountain. "One of these years, dudes, we'll ski it too," I said to the group.

The others had seen enough and pushed on. They were keen to find our slightly less extreme run off Russet Ridge—our main objective for the day. Again, I lingered behind. I was mesmerized by Fissile's rocky cliffs that were framed by long shoots of pristine white snow. I stood in silence, taking multiple pictures with the camera on my phone. A raven flew by as I was zipping my phone back into my coat. I remembered back to the beginning of the week and my new journal, with the raven and the eagle on the cover. The raven symbolized knowledge and wisdom. I wondered why it had flown by in that moment. Where was the wisdom in its presence? What knowledge was the raven trying to share? I watched it soar back to the west, while I gathered the last of my gear and followed the others off to the east.

I caught up to them soon after. They had stopped and were studying a topographic map, trying to locate our elusive run. Some of us had skied the same run a few years earlier and were convinced it was farther to the east, so we kept traversing in that direction. Half an hour later, with the sun getting lower in the sky, it was obvious that we weren't going to find it. We settled on another nearby descent that proved to be just as fun.

At the bottom of the run we put on our climbing skins to begin the long trek back towards the ski resort. On the return climb, we accidentally came across the run we had originally wanted to ski. So much snow has fallen that year that the ridge had transformed from a series of rocky cliffs, into a large white mound with only a few rocks poking through. The run, as we had known it from years previous, had completely transformed and was located west from where I had seen the raven. I realized the raven had been trying to tell me that we were going the wrong way. I was disappointed I hadn't been able to tap into the animal's knowledge. My spiritual game had a lot of room for improvement.

The next day I opted out of another trip up the mountain with the others, and instead spent the morning alone in the village. I put on my running shoes and headed towards the snow-covered Alta Lake. When I reached the lake, I was stoked to find that the snow on the surface of the frozen lake was just firm enough to run on. While thousands of skiers were crowded up on the resort mountains, I had the lake to myself.

I made my way onto the lake and broke into a slow run; landing my feet softly to avoid breaking through the top crust of snow. I was confident in the thickness of the ice below the snow, but also trusting that if I did go through, hopefully someone on shore would come to my rescue. I kept on running, as softly as I could. The sun was shining brilliantly. The lake was dead quiet, the only sound was my breathing as I ran. Just like I had felt all week, I continued to feel at peace. I was running, I was in nature, I was feeling the sun after months of walking the streets in the cold, dark, rain. I wasn't replaying the past. I wasn't worrying about the future, about what I was going to do about my job, or where and when I'd be ready for my next relationship. I was on the lake under the glow of a deep blue sky, breathing in the fresh mountain air. I was being present. I was at peace.

I caught an early afternoon bus back to Vancouver. Once in the city, I made a stop by the condo to drop off my ski gear. By early evening I was in the Olympic Village, ready to see my wife for the first time in months. I arrived early to our planned meeting spot: the giant bird sculptures in the middle of the main square. I wasn't nervous about what was going to happen between us, but it was going to be unfamiliar to see her again, after so much time. This was territory neither of us had been to before. I saw her approach, walking at her usual quick pace.

We said hello and exchanged a quick hug. She mentioned she was cold (at least that hadn't changed), so we walked to a nearby café so she could get a tea. Afterwards, we walked the short distance towards the manmade Habitat Island, which was not actually an island. "You know what this is called?" I asked her, as we walked the section of rocks that connected the mainland to the island.

"Let me guess, is it one of your favourite words?" she asked.

"Ha, you got it. It's a tombolo," I said, using a term I had learned years earlier studying coastal engineering.

"Nerd alert," she joked.

"Ha!"

It was good to meet in person, to see each other's body language, to laugh again at our inside jokes. We found a log to lean against on the rocky beach. I gave her space to do most of the talking in the beginning. She wanted to share the realizations and clarity that she had uncovered. The separation had been a catalyst for her awakening as well. We were both learning and growing, and simultaneously getting back to who we really were. We were undergoing a metamorphosis, to return to our true selves, before the layers of life, society and expectations masked our inner beings. We were both trying to figure out who we were and what we wanted. In the process, our souls' deepest desires would be revealed.

During our relationship we had been two incomplete halves trying to piece together to create a whole. I could be stubborn, arrogant, egotistic—not in a horrible beast sort of way, but I was at times, misguided. I had a big heart and big ambition, but never knew how to properly direct it. She had tried a few different career pursuits before falling in love with wildlife biology. Now she was obsessed. It was great to see, but I would never have a similar level of passion for the birds. We were both still evolving, the only question from my perspective was if we were evolving closer together, or farther apart. Our individual journeys could not be influenced in any direction, they were too important to both of our long-term happiness.

For the first hour I thought maybe there was a chance. Maybe we could get past what had *happened* and somehow find a way to get our life back together. The conversation was good. She was sharing, I was sharing, we were both talking about things like the Universe, manifesting, positive affirmations, seeing and thinking differently. Then she got lured back into trying to explain the past. She still felt that she needed to try and explain what had happened and why she'd made the choices she had. As if by reliving the past she could somehow convince me, or herself, that the right decisions had been made. I'd heard it all before. From my perspective there was no point trying to rehash what had happened or why everything unfolded the way it did. Nothing could be undone, so what was the point? I started to doubt any hopes of a reconciliation, whether she had even entertained the thought or not. I couldn't picture a lifetime of trying to explain the past. I wanted to be in the here and now and moving towards an intentional future.

She had got clear on one thing: she didn't want to live in the city. She had grown up on a farm outside of Kamloops, a smaller city in the BC Interior. She had always been more comfortable in rural settings. Kingston, where I grew up, wasn't exactly a raging metropolis, but I had an equal affinity for the fast-paced life in the city, while also getting away deep into the backcountry for bouts of bliss. We had talked about one day moving to the country, with chickens, dogs, and white-picket fences. I had said I would, and I would have, I would have done anything for her, but I doubt if I would have been truly happy. We would never know. "I'm going to move back to Kamloops, for the spring," she said. "I think I'll be more comfortable there."

"That's a good idea," I said. "It'll be good to test that out."

"What do you think you'll do in the next couple months?" she asked.

"Well, I'll be in Victoria until the end of April, and then I'm hoping to take some time off to travel. Maybe go see my sister's new place in Nicaragua."

"That would be amazing."

"Yeah, I suppose."

It was hard to get too excited talking with your wife about travel plans that did not include her, but it was clear that our paths were diverging, and not coming back together. She was seeking a quiet, simple way of life. I wasn't sure exactly what I was after, but I sensed that it was going to be anything but quiet. So many turbulent emotions had been spinning me around for months. It was only within that past week or so, really since my first call with Brittany, that I felt perhaps I could bring the chaotic emotional convulsions under control and direct my energy in a more meaningful way. I had a lot of energy, I just needed to focus on where to put it.

We agreed that things would remain unchanged; we were still separated. She would move on to Kamloops. I would go back to Victoria and then off traveling. I knew I wouldn't see her again before I left. It was clear we weren't going to try and get back together. Neither of us had tried to initiate that. A part of me wondered what would have happened if she'd wanted to give us another try. I hadn't planned how I would react to that. I just didn't know if I could even consider it. In some ways, we were both on the same page, both more focused on our own self development.

We got up off the log that we'd been sitting on. The sky had darkened, and it was starting to cool down. We slowly made our way back to where her car was parked. On the walk we talked briefly about getting the separation agreement started. Something neither of us wanted to consider, but something that had to be done. We agreed to try and get it done in April, before I left to travel.

We stopped by her car and hugged before she got in. This was it, really it. We had both cried over the course of the night. She shed a few more tears now during our embrace. We had met when we were so young, she was twenty-two and I was twenty-five. Over twelve years had passed since I first saw her at that pub in Victoria. I remembered being instantly electrified by the beauty of her eyes and her smile. There had been so much passion in the early years, as we crafted our life together. "I'm going to do my masters and then we're going to live in Vancouver, in a super nice apartment," I had said, during our first summer together. A year and half later that dream had become a reality.

We had continued to build our life together accomplishing our shared dreams of getting married, of traveling, of building our careers. But somewhere along the way our dreams got blurred. Our original shared dreams became less inspiring; talks of massive Vancouver mortgages and starting a family seemed to reach beyond the level of commitment that our relationship could handle. It was time that we both got back to who we really were, on a soul level. It was time that we both faced our own darkness so that we could move forward into the light. That was a journey that could not be done together.

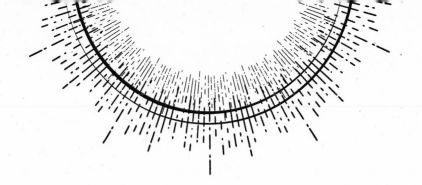

CHAPTER 9

CONNECTION

Connection is what happens when human beings spend time together without their thinking getting in the way.

MICHAEL NEILL

Monday morning, I made my way back to Victoria by float plane. The loft I was staying in was a short walk from the float plane terminal in the inner harbour. I dropped off my gear from the weekend and changed into my work clothes: long underwear top and bottom, grease-covered jeans, steel-toed boots, fleece top and waterproof jacket. As the engineer on-site I wasn't directly involved in any of the dirty work but encountering varying sources of grime was inevitable on the barge. I was changed and out the door within twenty minutes. The day passed with little excitement. After work I stopped to get groceries on my way back to the loft. I had been looking forward to a quiet night after a few days on the move.

After dinner I settled in on the couch with my latest book, Sebastian Junger's, *Tribe*[7]. I read how Junger described the three basic things humans need to be content: to be confident at what they do, to be authentic in their lives, and to be connected to one another. I put the book down to reflect on this. I had always been confident in most parts of life, with one exception. As an engineer I felt that my confidence was capped since my interest was limited: I was never going to be the world's best engineer, because there were more than a few aspects of the job that I wasn't passionate about. At the start of my career, the job also dampened my ability to be authentic; or rather, I restricted my authenticity when in the workplace. But I had made progress in previous years, especially over the past six months. It was the connection to others that gave me the most pause. I was connected to others, wasn't I? I wondered.

I didn't know if I was an introvert or extrovert; I had taken a behavioural test at some point, but the results didn't mean much to me. I had always enjoyed time with my friends. I was fortunate to have a tight crew from high school that had stayed in touch over the years. I developed another group of friends during university and we stuck together after graduation when we all moved on to start careers. When I first moved to Vancouver, I lucked into another crew to share ski, surf, and bike adventures with. I was overflowing with amazing buddies.

Once Rebecca and I got married, I naturally started to spend less time with 'the boys'. When the marriage ended, this became painfully obvious to me. For the most part, everyone was coupled-up by then. Just because I was newly single didn't mean we were going to start

---

7 Junger, Sebastian. *Tribe: On Becoming and Belonging.* Twelve, 2016.

hanging out multiple nights a week, like in the old days. As unfamiliar as it was to be alone, it was necessary. I needed the time, the space, the silence to think about what had happened, about who I was, and about where I was going next.

I had drifted away over the years from some friends. But immediately following the breakup, a new level of connection had emerged with deep conversations with new acquaintances. These were connections and conversations at a level I had never experienced. There was no small talk, and sometimes there was no talk at all, only a connection by being present with one another. It was these meaningful connections that I had chosen to work on during the long days on the job site.

The next morning on-site I was picked up from the small wooden dock that provided access from shore. Shawn, one of the workers, was relegated to be pick me up in his aluminum work boat. He was working on-site with his brother Cam. They were the two First Nations assistants working alongside the rest of the contractor's crew.

Cam was the taller and trimmer of the two. He brought an abundance of positivity and an even greater abundance of stories to site each day. His challenge was finding a willing audience to listen to his tales. Shawn was like me in a way, or like I had been over the previous few months. He seemed to be riding an erratic wave of joyful highs and sorrow-filled lows. He had an additional element of a hot temper added to his lows. That was something that I used to have, but for the most part, had been successful at shedding. I found Shawn to be the most interesting of the crew.

"Good morning, brother. Beautiful day, isn't it?" I said to Shawn, as I jumped into his boat.

"Ya, I guess," he said. I could tell he was in one of his funks. "Are you going straight to the barge?"

"Um, not quite yet, my man. Why don't we take a little cruise first?" I said.

"Sounds good to me. Where to?" he asked.

"Have you seen the eagles over on Inskip Island?"

"No, I haven't."

"Let's head that way."

We slowly made our way through the bay towards the island. It was still early in the morning; the air was fresh, a couple of degrees above freezing and pungent from the salty, nutrient-rich, cold ocean water that was brimming with sea life. As we boated farther out into the harbour the sun began to crest over the tall fir trees that lined the rocky shore. The slightest warmth touched our backs as we motored through the dark waters. Shawn didn't explain his mood; I didn't press him on it either.

"Check out that beauty!" I said to Shawn, as I pointed towards an eagle perched on one of the island's trees.

"Oh ya, she's a beauty. Here, take a look with the binoculars," Shawn said, passing them to me while inching the boat closer to the island. A smile had started to form across his face, one that wasn't present when he first picked me up.

We sat in silence, bobbing in the boat. We were staring at the eagle, that was also staring at us. The sun continued its slow climb higher in the sky. As it rose, it warmed all the organics that lived within the intertidal zone surrounding the rocky island. The sponges, the clams, the sea stars, the seaweed, the kelp, all of it coming more to life with each new ray of sun. It was nature at its best. "What a beautiful morning," Shawn said.

"It truly is, my man. It truly is," I said.

We motored slowly through the waters completing a turn around the west end of the island. The snow-capped Olympic Peninsula mountains came into view, across the Juan de Fuca Strait. The air was calm, so the surface of the ocean was as flat as a pancake. We were fully in the moment, connected to each other, while also connected to nature. Time was standing still, except it wasn't; I had to get to the barge and start work.

"Thanks, man. That was a great start to the day," Shawn said, as he positioned the boat alongside the barge.

"No, thank you, brother. Thanks for the ride. Thanks for the tour."

"Anytime, Mike, anytime," Shawn said, as he slowly pulled away in his boat, the same boat that he would work alone in for the remainder of the day. I couldn't know for sure, as he didn't say as much, but I sensed that our nature tour had helped lift his spirits. I knew for me it had been a memorable start to the day.

Later that night, back at the loft, I got set up on the couch to start working on the homework Brittany had given me. In the days since our first call, I had spent some time in my mind thinking about how I wanted my life to look ten years out. But what did I really want? It was a simple question, but it wasn't. My canvas was overwhelming blank. Seemingly, I could put whatever I wanted on it. In the past, I had given some thought towards future goals, but at the same time, they were never clearly defined. I had had a blurry vision of where my previous life was going before the separation, but I had never really sat down and consciously spent time thinking about what future I wanted to create.

I struggled to get started with the exercise. How could I possibly know what I wanted ten years out, when I barely knew how to get through the next few months? I thought back to what Brittany had said about focusing not as much on the *what* I wanted, for this first draft of long-term goals, but rather how I wanted to *feel* a decade into the future. That was easier: I wanted to feel incredible.

Brittany had given me six categories to work with. I started on the first: Health. A decade out I wanted to be one hundred percent healthy, feeling stronger and younger than ever before, injury and illness free. I didn't have any specific goals to put down, but I knew I wanted to continue with the sports I loved: yoga, surfing, biking, skiing, and I wanted to be doing them at a higher level than ever before. In all areas of my health, I wanted to be continuously improving and developing.

The next category was Relationships. One word instantly came to mind: I wanted all my relationships to feel *real*. The deeper connections I had been experiencing over the previous months, even if many of them were fleeting moments, had been meaningful. They had been true, real, connections gazing deeply into each other's eyes. These were the collection of moments I wanted in my life.

In many instances, these connections were easier with strangers. In the future, I knew I wanted to extend these meaningful interactions to family and friends. That was going to be a challenge. It was a good thing I had a decade to achieve that goal. I had no idea how I was going to bridge the safe distance that I had always kept with those closest to me. All the talk about the weather, or sports, or complaining about everything under the sun; had I always defaulted to those because I had been uncomfortable talking about anything with more depth? Was I afraid that my insecurities would be revealed, and I'd respond with a hot temper to protect myself? I wondered. This was going to be hard, but I believed I could do it, especially since I had already started having real conversations with others.

I wanted this same deep connection with my future partner. Over the previous months I had been getting clearer on me; on who I was. Through this process I was also getting much clearer on what type of partner I wanted to have. Rebecca and I had a good connection in the beginning. I couldn't remember for sure, but we must have talked about our future life together. Over the years that faded. Did we run out of things to talk about? Did we slowly find each other less interesting? I couldn't be sure. After our reunion the week before, it was now clear that my future wasn't going to include her as a partner. I knew I wanted to connect deeply, emotionally, spiritually, sexually with my future partner. I wanted to stay up late into the night talking about the Universe. I wanted to dream aloud about the life we would be creating, where we would travel, how we would grow old together.

I was also becoming very clear that I wanted to have kids. I couldn't explain it, but somehow, by having my heart broken, I had a stronger desire than ever to have kids. It was a though I knew that the gateway to rebuilding a stronger heart was to achieve the ultimate level of love by having kids of my own. I wanted that feeling of unconditional love that I had seen other parents have towards their children.

Next on Brittany's list was Career. The first word that came to mind was: flourishing. I had always had the drive and determination, my biggest challenge in my career was that I could never find an outlet that I was inspired enough to pour all my energy into. At many times over my engineering career I had felt stagnant, bored. I had never felt anything close to flourishing. I had no idea in what I would be flourishing in ten years' time, but I knew I wanted it. I also knew that I wanted to be doing fulfilling work that I loved. I need to find that sweet spot that didn't feel like work at all.

The next thing on the list was Contribution: how I wanted to give back to the world. I was starting to think boldly by this point in the list, so I put down that I wanted to change people's lives. Several times over the previous months I had shared with others what I had been going through and all that I was learning. On a few occasions I would witness friends have instantaneous shifts in their perspective; they would have an "ah-ha" moment right in front of me. It was as though I could see a new concept landing in their mind. It was never my intention to convince them of anything, I was just sharing from my heart. It was powerful to see my words impact others. I could see it in their eyes, that I had helped change them, in a positive direction. I didn't yet know what to do with this or how to apply it, but I knew I could figure it out and contribute at a higher level.

A theme of flexibility drove my goals for Money & Abundance; the next item on the list. In ten years' time, my goal was to live where I wanted, travel when I wanted, eat what I wanted, and do it all without having to worry about money. I wasn't focused on a dollar amount, a size of house, or a type of car (I didn't even have a *thing* for cars). It had never been about chasing a number. But I did want me and my future family to be comfortable. I wanted us to be able to enjoy all of life's amazing experiences, and that would take money.

Finally, for Mindset and Consciousness (the last item on Brittany's list), I wanted to be continuously evolving, myself. Really, I had only just started working on myself. I had always worked on my body through exercise, but I had never really worked on my mind, on my limiting beliefs, on the shadows in my soul. My transformation started when I first started to become conscious of myself. The whole concept of consciousness was so new to me that, in the beginning, I had to Google what the heck it meant. Once I had begun to explore further developing myself, which I later learned was called personal development (which seemed to make sense), I started hearing terms like *shadow work, inner child, and manifesting*. The separation had also been the catalyst to introduce me to meditation. It had been a great tool to attempt to release all the negative things that had been passing through my mind. But I had a long way to go with the meditation, and all the inner work. I had only just started scratching the surface of trying to understand ancient spiritual teachings. I wanted to fully explore any available wisdom, and I wanted to use it to develop myself, and others.

Below the list that I had been recording in my journal, I added one final goal that I wanted to be feeling in ten years' time. Just like my New Year's resolution, I wanted to continue to be present. Like all the new terms that were becoming part of my vocabulary, this one also took some time to fully understand. What did it mean to be fully present? I wondered. For me, it had been the times when I was in nature when I was fully present. I'd be staring at a mountain, or the Pee Tree, or an eagle, and I would completely lose track of time. I was still working on achieving this same thing during my meditations, by focusing on my breath as it went in and out. There was still much work to be done, but I had got a sense of how powerful being present could be. When I was fully present, I wasn't thinking about the breakup that was in the past, or the uncertainty of my future, I was only existing in the Now. And in the Now, very rarely was anything lacking.

My homework was complete. In creating the list, I hadn't worried about the *how* or the *what* that would be required to achieve the goals. I had simply put trust in the Universe (another new concept I was getting used to) that if I had clear intentions, and took the appropriate action, my goals could be achieved.

I put down the journal and lay back on the couch. My mind danced with images of my future life. There were still so many unknowns, but it didn't matter, because I had the feeling. I had the feeling that I wanted in my future life. A feeling that I was already feeling in the Now. A feeling that felt a lot better than what I had been feeling over the past several months.

———————

St Patrick's Day passed slowly on-site. Since it was a Saturday, we only worked a half day under the brilliant March sunshine. I texted Brittany to tell her I had completed my homework. I had hoped my coach would be proud.

"Hi, I finished my homework. My ten-year goals. Feels good to have it done, to have it down on paper," I texted.

"Awesome. Proud of you. Great start," she wrote back immediately.

"Thanks. It was a good exercise."

"Are you ready for what's next?"

"Ya, for sure."

"Okay, I want you to journal about these three things: your biggest Fears, Insecurities, and Excuses, that are holding you back from achieving your goals."

"Yikes. Okay, I'll try."

"You'll try?"

"I mean, I'll get it done."

"Now we're talking."

Once I got back to the loft after work, I headed out for a run along the inner harbour. After the run I took a quick shower, then parked myself on the couch to spend Saturday night working on my next piece of homework.

It was easy to identify my biggest fear; it was that I would not achieve greatness, that I would not reach my full potential. My biggest fear was that I would live an average, comfortable, safe, and boring life. As I wrote this in my journal, I realized to an extent that was how I had been living in my old life. There had been elements of excitement, but I had always operated from a place of trying to keep things safe: staying within my comfort zone, trying to avoid surprises, and working hard not to upset anyone. It was at times a mundane way to exist. I realized that by playing it safe, I was unconsciously reinforcing my biggest fears. By staying within my comfort zone, I was inhibiting the very greatness that I had always wanted to achieve.

I cringed deeply as I moved on to insecurities. Taking a deep breath, I landed on the one thing that had always been nagging me: my height. At five foot seven I was no basketball player, and a few inches below average. Writing this out I realized just how ridiculous it was to let something I had no control over dictate how I felt. By addressing this insecurity straight on, I seemed to release it once and for all.

Lastly, I thought about what excuses I had that could hold me back from achieving my goals. I lay back on the couch and smiled, I had none. I had nothing holding me back from working towards achieving all my goals and creating the life I wanted. I realized that it wasn't the marriage that had previously held me back, rather, it was myself: my fears, insecurities and excuses, my lack of focus on what I really wanted, my desire to keep things safe and controlled. With that new clarity I was free to push myself to go after all that I wanted.

Sunday morning, I drove twenty minutes out of town to Ten Mile Point to meet a co-worker for some ocean kayaking. Matt, an avid paddler, generously lent me one of his boats, then guided us across the open water to the Chatham Islands. Returning to shore a couple of hours later, we pulled our boats out of the water and unpacked our gear. I had always been drawn to the water. Back when I was growing up in Kingston, I'd spent every summer on the water learning how to sail at summer camp. In high school I moved to teaching sailing at the camp and competing in regattas on the weekends. I'd travel all over Ontario with the racing team, sailing during the days and partying at night. I managed to excel at both the sailing and the partying. I made the national junior team and traveled to South Africa to represent Canada, while at the same time, balancing (at times successfully, at other times not) a few romances within the sailing community. They were great days and ever since I had always gravitated to the water.

Before he left, I convinced Matt to join me for a quick polar plunge in the frigid ocean waters. I had recently added cold water therapy to my wellness routine. Each day, I would end the last minute of every shower with the setting as cold as it would go. By ending cold, I was building resilience by training my brain not to back away from a challenge. I had learned that there were other benefits of cold-water therapy: fat loss, improved immunity, better circulation, reduced stress, increased testosterone, healthier skin and hair, improved sleep, plus the obvious one: an instant increase in alertness. It was a healthy, natural way to feel more alive and I rarely passed up an opportunity to jump in the water.

I made my way into the water and Matt followed soon after. He didn't last long. "That's cold, man!" he yelled, as he quickly retreated out of the ocean.

"The colder the better!" I said.

"You're crazy, man. How can you still be in there? How did you not scream when you got in?!" he asked.

"Ah, man. I've been training for this. I have a bit of an advantage. It's all in the breathing, you just have to slow your breathing down and focus on something else, something warmer," I said, still bobbing in the water. "It's just like Wim Hof does, you should check him out."

"Whatever, man, you and this Wim Hof guy are nuts."

"You'll come to love it. Afterall, how you show up in the cold is how you show up in life."

"Well, I guess I have some work to do."

Matt took off soon after to spend Sunday afternoon with his wife and kids. I had nowhere to be until dinner later that night at Jenn's. I grabbed my water bottle and set off to explore the rocky beach just beyond where we had launched our kayaks.

I didn't get far before I found a place to rest. I took a seat on the rocky beach leaning against a large piece of driftwood. I was tired after a full week of work. The mid-March sun was shining, giving off real warmth for the first time in months. The wind was light, blowing slightly offshore out of the cove. Gentle wavelets lapped rhythmically against the kelp-covered rocks. Shore birds darted between the arbutus tress that traced the shore. I had the empty cove to myself. It was bliss, until my phone lit up with a series of incoming messages over social media. From the profile that accompanied the messages, I saw they were coming from a girl named Anne.

"Are you a real person? You ride road bikes. You've done triathlons, meditate, and go to counseling," she wrote. She had originally found me through a meditation app which showed other people who were meditating in your area at the same time. The intent of the app's feature was to show a collective consciousness of people meditating at the same time. I had linked one of my social media accounts to my profile on the app. I assumed that Anne must have spent some time going through my social media feed to learn more about me. Ever since the separation I had started to share more of myself online. It was a means for me to express all the new thoughts I was having and what I was learning. I had shared more vulnerably than ever before, including a post on how I had gone to see a counselor. Subconsciously, I had also been sharing more to perhaps attract my next partner. After receiving the messages from Anne, I wondered if it was starting to work.

"Yes, I'm super real," I typed.

We messaged back and forth about meditation, Ironman races, and past struggles. It seemed we had a lot in common. I shared about my separation and she shared about a hard end to her last relationship. She was studying social work, so she was a good resource to be open with.

"I think it takes a lot of resilience to learn and grow, it's a big courageous move," she wrote, referring to the personal development journey I had begun. "Not everyone wants to do it, it's easier to self-medicate."

I had been *doing the work*, but I had never thought of it as courageous. More so, I was just doing what I had always done, trying to figure things out. On the other hand, I didn't tell her about how much more I had drank in the beginning, or about how the hangovers had been getting progressively worse. But still, I received the compliment since I had been doing better recently. In fact, I hadn't had a bad day in weeks. "I honestly feel like I have superpowers sometimes. The alone time, the space, the meditation, it's been amazing to help me find clarity."

She was based in Vancouver, so I mentioned that I wasn't going to be back for at least a couple months, as I had to finish my work in Victoria, then I was going traveling.

"That's probably a good thing," she wrote. "You don't want to meet me."

"Of course I do!"

"If I'm going to be honest, I'm a bit freaked out to meet you, because we seem to have a lot of similarities."

"You're right. Better to play it safe and never meet."

"Are you poking fun!?"

"You bet." I responded, smiling as I typed it out. "I did have a thought this morning, during my meditation. I saw myself, sometime soon, backstage at a concert. Then I had a separate vision where I was wearing something new and amazing while being photographed by an aspiring young photographer. It was all super cool, it felt good."

"I'll see what I can do," she joked.

"I'll be waiting patiently."

"What's the most painful part of dealing with the separation from your wife?"

"Honestly, lately, there hasn't been too much. Early on, it was a different story. The fear of being lonely forever, and just the disbelief that she had chosen a new path in life, that didn't include me."

"How long were you married?"

"Married six years, together for twelve. We didn't communicate well, we lost the connection, developed different dreams. Over the past couple months, we've both been working hard to uncover our true selves. As we've got closer to doing this, it seems as though perhaps we weren't right for each other after all. I'm starting to see that maybe it was a good thing to have it all blow up."

"What do you think was your part in the demise of it all?"

"Not knowing how to communicate. I didn't know how. I'm working hard on that now. Speaking of which, if I'm going to be honest, I must get going. I'm going to dinner at my sister's."

"I appreciate you letting me know. It's been a pleasure to chat."

"The pleasure is all mine," I replied, smiling.

A few days later, on Wednesday night, I met my buddy Jake for a healthy dinner at Rebar, a restaurant downtown in Bastion Square. The last time I had seen him was in November in Vancouver. The separation had been so fresh at that time, it had only been a few weeks. I remembered that after I had met him that day, I had walked across downtown to meet my counselor. It seemed like so much had happened since that time; I had processed so many emotions, most of which were painful. As I made the short walk from the loft to the restaurant, I reflected on the person who I was in that moment, compared to the manic, tired, confused, scared, lonely person I was back in November. There was no way to measure just how much progress I had made, but I knew for certain that to an extent I had pulled myself out of that November rock bottom. We had a lot to catch up on.

We arrived around the same time and were led to a table near the back of the restaurant. Jake was in town to take his work clients to a concert. I sensed he had plenty on his mind with a wife, two young kids, and a job that had him traveling around the province. Despite that, he was curious to know how I was holding up.

"So, how are you doing?" Jake asked, after we had taken our seats and ordered our food and drinks.

"I'm actually feeling fairly good these days. I've been over here in Victoria for about a month and a half. It totally sucked in the beginning. I thought that everything would change and get easier just by moving here. Turns out that thought was a misguided one," I said.

"Wherever you go, there you are," said Jake.

"Exactly. I was still stuck in my head. February was tough: I cried a lot. But I kept going and processing all the crap that came up, just moving forward each day. I kept on thinking that if something external, like the breakup, could send me into such an emotional pit, then why couldn't *I* do something to spin myself back in the other direction to get happy again?"

"I sort of follow you, man."

"I know, it's hard to explain. All I know is that I just kept thinking about what I was thinking about. When what I was thinking about was painful, I thought about why it was painful. If it was a hard truth that I had to realize, then I accepted that—as painful as it sometimes was—and moved on. At the same time, when I'd have moments of clarity, or when I was feeling good being fully present, I thought about that, and why that was feeling good. Basically, I've just been paying attention to what I've been thinking about, and by doing so I've slowly started to shift from thinking about all the pain from the past or the unknowns in the future, to instead just being more present. And let me tell you, that has helped a lot."

"You've been talking to Max, haven't you?" Jake snickered.

"Ha-ha, ya, man, he loves this stuff."

"Well, you look better, my brother, you look good. We were all worried about you. We care about you."

A silence lingered between us as I received Jake's compliment. It felt good to have that little piece of validation, that I was making progress, despite how hard things had been.

"Thank you, brother," I said. "How about you, what's new?"

"I'm good, man, except my work wants me to consider a position in Calgary."

"Cowtown, eh, what's the family think about that?"

"They're not keen, I mean I don't really want to move either, we're set up well in Vancouver. But it's a good opportunity, so we'll see."

"Ya, man, that's a full province over. That would be a big change."

"Absolutely."

"How's Steph doing with Carter?" I asked about his wife and their new baby boy.

"Great!" he said, before going quiet.

"All the travel I do for work, it gets hard you know. In fact, last week when I was away, I realized for the first time that I was lonely."

I'd always been envious of Jake's work travel, which had him on the road at least a few days each week. It always seemed like a great job. But despite the successful career, he found himself wanting to be home with his wife and kids. He went on to tell me how, when he got back home, he shared these feelings with his wife when they sat down for a relationship check-in.

"I just told her straight up that that week had been pretty hard, because I had wanted to be home with her and the kids. I also asked her how she was doing, with all my travel. She told me that it was also hard for her, having me away so much. But she also said that 'it was what it was' and they'd just have to keep communicating to make it work."

"That's amazing, man. You guys really have a good thing going, a true partnership."

"Ya, we're lucky. And to be honest, after seeing what you and Rebecca went through, we've been checking in more with each other lately. Just to talk through whatever crap is going on. It's been good, man."

"I love that, it's so simple."

"And then the sex!" Jake whispered, "After that conversation, we had the best sex we've ever had!"

"I love it!" I said, as we leaned back in our chairs, bellies full of laughter. As our laughter died down, the server came by with our meals. "So, what about you, man, any thoughts about dating again?" Jake asked.

"Oh god. Ya, of course I've thought about it—about how I hope to just skip it. You know me, I always sucked at dating," I said.

"Ah, come on, man, you dated girls when we were in university."

"Ya, sort of, but that was like fifteen years ago. I can't even imagine how different things are now, apparently it's all done over apps—what the heck is that?"

"Ah, you'll be fine. You're a good-looking guy, you'll do great, it'll be fun."

"Dude, not all of us are good at dating, like you were back in the day. I think I'll just skip it."

"Skip it? How exactly is that gonna work?"

"Hear me out. I think I'm on to something. It's weird, the more I've been working on myself these last few months, the more I've gotten clarity on what sort of partner I'm looking for."

"Makes sense."

"Ya, so I figure I can just skip a bunch of drawn-out dating with multiple women, because I will have an instant knowing when I meet The One."

"I don't know, man, but if you say so. So just what does The One look like?"

"Confident. Ambitious. Honest. Energetic. Independent. Committed. Basically, my Queen."

"Sounds perfect, do you think you can find her?"

"Ah, well, I may have already."

"What?!"

"Well, it's not like that. Um, this is different. You see, I've hired a coach, and she kind of fits that description."

"A coach?"

"Ya, like a life coach."

"Hmm, I've never heard of a life coach."

"Ya, I guess it's kind of a new thing. You've heard of Tony Robbins, right?"

"Ya."

"Ya, sort of like him. Someone to motivate you, someone to help you move forward, someone to help you see your blind spots, overcome limiting beliefs, help with goal setting. Basically, someone to help accelerate your life and your growth."

"Hmm, sounds sweet. And so, you've hired a coach who just happens to resemble your perfect partner?"

"No! But, I mean, maybe. Here, just see for yourself," I said, as I pulled my phone out of my pocket and scrolled to Brittany's social media profile.

"My word, man, she's gorgeous," said Jake.

"Ya, ya she is. But that's beside the point. She's a great coach; she's a badass. She whips my ass into shape, calls me on my crap. We've only just started working together and already I feel different, more confident, more focused. I certainly feel a heck of a lot better than the past few months."

"Well all that sounds wicked. I'm happy for you. Just maybe try not to fall for your coach."

"Ha, ya, I'll try."

After we paid our bills, we made our way through the restaurant and out to the street. Jake headed off to his hotel and I headed the opposite direction back to the loft. As I walked through Victoria's historic downtown, I thought about dinner with Jake and how good it felt to talk. We had been out to dinner many times before, but we had never talked about feeling lonely; we had never talked about how we were struggling. Being guys, we had always kept those topics buried under multiple layers of sports, or the dreaded weather talk. I had always thought that being vulnerable and sharing about struggles meant that I was weak. But after dinner with Jake, and other conversations over the previous months, I was feeling the opposite—that by being vulnerable I was showing courage, and by showing courage, I was building deeper connections. All of that, as hard as it was at times, felt really damn good.

Crossing Pandora Street on the way to the loft, I noticed for the first time the historic business name painted directly above the loft windows where I had been staying. It read: "Hip Lung Co.". I took this as a sign: *Hip*, as in my favourite band, The Tragically Hip, as in the lead singer and my hero, Gord Downie. Gord had been with me the whole time I had been in Victoria. It was the first time since my experience on New Year's Eve with the distorted lightshow on my phone, that I had really felt the synchronicities of the Universe. I had firmly believed that the word Hip, over the loft where I had lived for the past month and a half, symbolized that through his spirit, Gord had looked over me and instilled in me some of the very wisdom that had made him my hero in the first place. I believed that, I felt that, I knew that, and I didn't have to get any of it validated by anyone. That feeling was mine and it made me feel alive.

Once I was up in the loft, I brushed my teeth and got ready for bed. Once in bed, I journaled about the day's events. As I was journaling, my mind drifted back to something else that Brittany had mentioned to me: that I should tell my story. I had resisted at the time, to which she replied that I was more than a little stubborn—which was accurate—but like most things, Brittany had suggested, I had eventually come around to consider the idea. I hadn't thought about telling my story or writing a book in weeks. I returned to the same blocks that had come up when I had first considered the idea: who would care and what would be the point? I still didn't have those answers.

I did know that a transformation had occurred. After months of living with a darkened soul, I had slowly started to crawl out and see some light. On top of that, the Me that was crawling out of the dark hole was not the same Me that had entered the cave in the first place. I had changed, evolved, and I felt it was for the better. Maybe there was someone out there who was in a similar dark place, who could be inspired by the progress I was making. Maybe I could help them by telling my story. I wondered. Still, I couldn't write a book, that wasn't in my skillset—I was an engineer; I did numbers, not words.

Lying in bed I returned to an older thought. Maybe I could have someone else write my story. Who could I send my growing volume of journals and have them turn the words into a book? Who could I trust with this important project? Who did I know who could write? Seb, I knew Seb. My friend since childhood. My strong friend who had beaten Leukemia as a teenager. My friend who I had serendipitously seen on that fateful trip home to Kingston at Christmas. Seb was a writer, and a damn fine one. Seb could help make this happen. Seb could be the one to bring this story to life. Before I closed my eyes on the day, I grabbed my phone and emailed her my idea.

Soon after, I drifted off to sleep dreaming of telling my story through Seb's writing, for all the world to read.

The next night, Jake and I met downtown to share a taxi to the concert. He had extended the invite to me, to attend as one of his guests. "I could have sworn you were going to bail. I know how much you love country music," Jake said sarcastically, as we got into the taxi.

"I'd be lying if I said the thought hadn't crossed my mind," I said.

"Ha!"

"I'm actually excited. I'm looking forward to this. I've been wanting to start doing new things, have more new experiences, what better place to start than a little hoedown music."

"Ah, come on, it's not like it's a barn dance, this guy rocks out!"

"Who is it, again?"

"His name is Brett Kissel, he's Canadian. You've never heard of him?"

"Negative. I had meant to look him up before tonight but didn't make it a priority."

"It's all good. You'll know him after tonight, especially since we have backstage passes. We get to meet him before the show!"

"Get out! That's awesome." As I spoke the words, my mind wandered back to what I had said to Anne, a few days earlier, when I had told her about my vision of being backstage at a concert. A vision that was about to come true. I wondered, if by speaking and sharing my visualization, I had helped to make it happen.

After a twenty-minute ride we arrived at the venue. Once inside, Jake and I, along with his clients, were ushered into a small side room for our backstage experience. Our group, along with about thirty others, gathered in an awkward semicircle while we waited for Brett to enter the room.

"Hey, everyone, so great to see you!" Brett said, to a quiet applause when he finally entered. The applause faded, and Brett said a few words. He was beaming. Where other performers might see a depressing sideroom of a small-town community centre filled with only a handful of fans, Brett gave off nothing but gratitude to be part of that moment. He made eye contact with everyone in the room as he ran through a thank you list which included his crew, his fans, and his family. Following his talk, he took time for photos with each one of us. "That guy is going to be famous one day," I said to Jake. "He's got the right vibe."

After Brett left the room, we all made our way into the theatre for the start of the concert. Once the show got started, I found myself enjoying the upbeat country music. I wasn't about to go out and buy a cowboy hat, but I was on my feet with the rest of the crowd. But halfway through the show something felt off. I told Jake that I needed to get some air and headed outside.

When I got outside, I slowly circled around the entrance fountain, trying to figure out why I was feeling off for the first time in weeks. Instead of trying to fight the pain, I thought deeply about why I'd sunk into that state, and what the Universe was trying to tell me. "What is it?" I said repeatedly, gazing up into the dark sky.

Shifting my focus to the statue in the middle of the fountain, I thought of Brett inside the theatre, commanding the audience, inspiring the crowd, unapologetically living his dream as a music star. In a moment of clarity, I knew what was bothering me: I wanted to be the one on stage. I wanted to be the one commanding the audience, inspiring the crowd. Deep down, I had always wanted that, but it had always come from the wrong place, it had always been about me. Now things were different, it was about them, it was about others. I could see how I could inspire others by sharing what I had been through and all that I was learning. I pulled my phone out of my coat pocket to text the one person who would understand: "I'm done being in the crowd, I want to be the one on stage."

A reply came back immediately: "YES," Brittany wrote in capital letters. She understood, she knew what had been unlocked within me. She knew that I was ready to connect with the world on a whole new level.

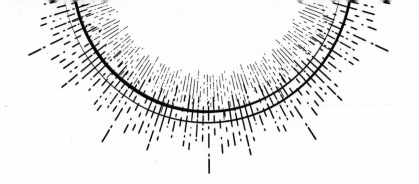

CHAPTER 10

DHARMA

The two most important days in your life are the day you were born and the day you find out why.

MARK TWAIN

A few days later, on Saturday morning, we achieved a project milestone on-site, completing the last of the dredging. It had taken the crew about two months to dredge out all the contaminated material. All that remained was to fill the hole with clean rock. The filling typically took about half the time as the dredging, so we were all hoping to be done with the project before the end of April. That was assuming everything went smoothly. I left the site around midday and headed back to the loft. At the loft, I spent some time outlining a work presentation I was preparing to give at an upcoming conference in Seattle.

Following my realization at the concert, I was viewing the conference presentation as my first step towards getting on bigger stages. I wanted to give a clear, concise, and impactful presentation. I knew if I were to have a future on stage, I would have to master the fundamentals of public speaking. I did some research online to learn everything I could about creating a profound talk. I learned how important it was to show your passion and tell a story. I read about how you want to teach the audience something new and create a *wow* moment. I knew that the engineering topic I was presenting wasn't my deepest passion or my life's purpose. I thought back to the law of dharma and how every person has a purpose in life and a special gift to share with others. I was still trying to get clear on what that was for me, but I did know that any stage was an opportunity to practice and get better. I was excited to get in the spotlight.

On Saturday night I went out for drinks with coworkers. On Sunday, I awoke with the consequential hangover. In a pulsing fog, my mind struggled to come to life—I had to stop doing this to myself. I had things I wanted to be doing, books I wanted to be reading, presentations I was excited to work on. All of it had to wait until my muddled mind was clear enough to concentrate. Despite my best intentions to drink less, I was struggling to find the balance between going out with friends, versus having a clear mind to continue with my personal growth.

I managed to drag myself to a yoga class mid-morning to work out some of the cobwebs in my head. Back at the loft after the class, my head was finally clear enough so that I could focus. I had some thoughts that I wanted to work through. I found my journal and started to write. It was becoming clear to me that I liked to help others work through their problems. Where others would be overwhelmed and unclear on certain aspects of their lives, I found that I was able to help them organize their mind and achieve some clarity. Maybe it was the engineer in me, was I engineering their minds? I didn't know. I also couldn't help but see the potential in others, that they were sometimes blind to. Where my friends or colleagues would get bogged down with limiting beliefs, excuses and doubt, I could clearly see if they could tweak their mindsets and apply a little more confidence, they would be able to move closer to achieving their dreams and reach their full potential. Plus, it was fun to help others see their challenges from a different perspective. If I was helping others and enjoying doing it, had I found my dharma?

As I journaled, I thought back to something else that Brittany had suggested to me: that maybe I too was a coach. She had been impressed at my ability to feel empathy for others, and based on my progress in personal development, she thought that not only could I be a coach, but I could be a great coach. At first, I had automatically dismissed it. Who was I to coach others? How would I know what to say? Would I be any good at it? I decided to leave it at that, with the questions unanswered for the time being. I would let the thought of becoming a coach marinate in the back of my mind.

Site work Monday morning started by backfilling the hole we had been digging for the past two months. We got halfway through the day before we were shut down by equipment failure. It wasn't a good start to the last portion of the project. I had to move out of the loft that night, so I took off early from the site to get a head start on packing. The loft had other tenants moving in, so I had been forced to find a new place to live for my final month in Victoria. I wanted to stay in the same neighbourhood since the historic buildings gave off great energy. I remembered that someone had told me that the historic Swans Hotel, just down the street, accepted long term guests.

I had taken a tour a few days earlier and decided on the large second floor, one-bedroom corner suite above the pub. The suite, the second largest in the hotel after the penthouse, was available at a reduced rate due to the length of my stay, and because of the noise from the pub below. Since it was an older wood-framed building, sound traveled easily between floors.

Later that evening, I started the first of multiple trips moving my stuff from the loft, down the street to the hotel. A woman greeted me at the hotel's front desk to begin the check-in process. "You know, most people don't choose that room, because of the noise," she reminded me, as I started the paperwork.

"How bad could it be?" I asked.

I had convinced myself I could deal with the noise, mainly because I had already fallen in love with the suite's high ceilings, Juliette windows and thick exposed beams. The size of the space was too good to pass up. I was sure I could find a way to manage the noise.

"For the most part it's not that bad. It just gets a little rowdy on Friday and Saturday nights. Don't say we didn't warn you," she said.

"I consider myself warned. I'll still take it."

"Alright sounds good, how do you spell your last name again?" she asked, as she filled out the last of the paperwork.

As I spelled out my last name, I had a thought—a beautiful thought. One day, I had no idea when, but one day, people would know my name. People would know who I was; they'd recognize my name and I wouldn't have to spell it out. I had never had that thought before, or if I had, I had never *believed* it would come true. In that moment, like never before, I believed in myself. I wasn't thinking from a place of ego, but rather from a place of knowing. I had experienced rock bottom, I had been with me at my worst, but I had managed to get out of that hole. Not only had I got out, but I seemed to be evolving to an even more peaceful existence than I was at before. I knew I had been through something and I knew it had been powerful. I also felt that I wanted to share my experiences with others because I knew it could help in a positive way. I just knew that one day, once I figured out how to teach what I had learned, people would know my name.

"It's T, R, A, N, as in November, M, as in Mike, E, R," I spelt it out patiently. One day I knew that scene would be different. With check in complete, I finished moving the last of my gear then got ready to spend my first night in the suite.

The contractor spent all day Tuesday working on repairs, so I had a day off from the site. I started the day with a run around the inner harbour. When I got back, I saw that I had a message from Anne, the girl I had met online through the meditation app. "Hey! Hope you're having a great week; thought you might like this Ted Talk," she wrote. With no pressing plans for the morning I clicked on the link and loaded the video.

The talk was by relationship expert, Esther Perel. The message of her talk was that we must stay true to ourselves and not let our partners take any of our identity. She mentioned that the period after breakups was a great opportunity for individuals to create their true selves and become happy simply being alone. That was certainly what I had been focused on doing. Instead, she went on, most people try to immediately seek out a partner to fill the void that exists after a breakup. That always backfires as the one partner becomes too reliant on the other for happiness, instead of generating it from within. The right approach was to be in a good space before starting a new relationship, as two individuals firmly grounded in who they were. It was key to maintain that space as separate identities throughout a relationship.

I paused the video and took a moment to reflect. That was where

Rebecca and I had gone wrong at the beginning of our relationship. Neither of us knew who we were. It was through no fault of our own, neither of us had had the life experiences, or the awareness, to establish that sense of self. We were young when we first got together: I was twenty-five and she was twenty-two; but we weren't *that* young. Whatever we were, neither of us could have been described as *firmly grounded*.

That lack of being firmly rooted in our sense of self meant that both of us had tried to take on the identity of the other at certain points throughout our relationship. I would try to force myself to be more interested in her passion for wildlife, while she would try to force herself into doing the extreme sports that I loved. We didn't know it at the time, but that was causing us to drift farther away from our true selves, which had only caused more internal stress.

Perel went on to describe how the benefit of being in a functional relationship was that each partner acts as a cheerleader for the other, encouraging the thoughts, values, and beliefs of the other, instead of trying to conform them closer to their own. The magic happens when both partners respect the other as an individual and continually encourage the other to learn, grow, and evolve into better versions of themselves. To me, it kind of sounded like having your own life coach for life.

_____

The contractor completed the repairs and we were back on-site for Wednesday and Thursday. Friday was a holiday, Good Friday, so on Thursday night I went out again with my co-workers. The night started with good intentions. Two of my co-workers, Erin and Markus, along with my buddy Justin, gathered in the suite for a few drinks in the early evening. I was excited to show off the new digs that I had moved into. Later, we moved downstairs to the pub for more drinks and a round of burgers. After that it was on to Saint Frank's for more drinks.

To her credit, Erin recognized that the night was going nowhere and was the first to leave. Justin was the next to bow out, also sensing that the night had peaked. Markus and I decided to push on, so we went to Fiamo, an Italian pizza and wine bar.

It was well after midnight when I found myself sitting next to a wasted university student. He slurred a bunch of words in my direction with a glazed look in his eyes. He was either going to punch me in the face or puke all over me. I didn't feel like sticking around to experience either. It was in that moment when I finally realized that I did not want to be there. Why was I still out, well after midnight, when nothing good ever happens? Was I looking for my future wife? Was I ready for that? Was I going to find her here, drunk, amongst a bunch of rowdies? Did I even want to meet my future Queen in such a place? Would she even be in such a place, at this time of night? I doubted it.

Friday morning brought with it a splitting headache and putrid beer-laced breath. I had so much I wanted to do that day: read my latest book, work on my presentation, journal about my thoughts. All my productivity, creativity and energy were on hold until my mind cleared, which wouldn't happen until the afternoon. It was a waste of a morning. I really, *really*, couldn't go on like that.

Brittany had been challenging me to see how much money I was spending on alcohol. But on that Good Friday morning, it became clear to me that it wasn't the wasted money that bothered me the most, it was the wasted time. I had too much that I was excited to do. I had to reclaim that time. I had to break a habit that no longer served me. On that Easter weekend, I said goodbye to something that had been so central to my life for so many years. I quit drinking.

———————

I woke up Saturday, the last day in March, feeling like a million bucks. After the previous day's debacle, I was ready to end the month with a productive day. As I was making breakfast, I read from my latest book purchase: *The Developing Mind*[8], by Dr. Daniel Siegel. I had been searching for a book that would help me better understand the changes that I had experienced in my mind. The book was helping, but it was dense. I still couldn't fully grasp all the teachings. I read that the mind was a process that regulates the flow of energy and information. "Energy and information, energy and information," I repeated to myself out loud. Of course, that's what the mind does, I thought, but what did that mean? And how did that help me understand what was going on with my mind? I still had a long way to go, and I was going to have to find a different book to help me.

After breakfast, I sat down at the dining room table to journal about a question that had been on my mind for a few days: how could people shift their lives without having to hit rock bottom? I had come to the realization that the separation, and all the pain that had come with it, was exactly what I had needed. Out the other side of the trauma was emerging a new me. I didn't know how it had happened; I couldn't

---

8 Siegel, Daniel J. *The Developing Mind: How Relationships and the Brain Interact to Shape Who We Are.* The Guilford Press, 2001.

explain why it had happened; all I knew was that something had shifted within me, for the better.

The new me had a multitude of facets. It was as though I was carrying a new confidence, a new fearlessness. I had started thinking bigger, dreaming bigger, because I knew if I failed, there was no failure that was going to feel worse than the trauma I had already survived. I was also learning how to more easily access peace, something that many strived for. I had spent a large part of my time since the separation simply trying to be happy again. I had worked on my thoughts through meditation, I had moved my body through yoga and other exercise, I had avoided negativity like the plague, and I had focused on being present. Slowly, it had started to work. Slowly, I had started to not only find that level of contentment I had before the breakup, but at times access a whole new dimension of bliss. In doing so, I realized how many others could benefit from a similar transformation. But I wondered, how could they access a similar shift without going through a trauma of their own?

I thought about how ever since arriving in Victoria, I had been having new experiences. I remembered that I had been disappointed when I first arrived, because I didn't instantly feel better. I was still with me, and my same head. But over the previous two months, I had made progress. I couldn't help but wonder if it had something to do with the new experiences I had been having. The changes weren't major, but they were still new to me. I was living in new places, I was shopping at new grocery stores, I was going to a new yoga studio, I was working at a new site, I was going to new coffee shops, I was meeting new people, I was running new routes. I couldn't help but wonder if all these experiences had played a role to help leave my old world behind. I was forging a new path and in doing so, awakening a part of my mind that had been asleep for so long. This could also be the key for others to change their lives: small changes and new experiences that compound to build a new path forward.

Around mid-morning I took a break and went for an oceanside run in the spring sunshine. Back in the suite after the run, I grabbed a water bottle and stepped onto the small balcony outside one of the Juliette windows. The energy was building as hundreds of people gathered across the street for the opening of a new bridge. I had the best view in town, as the mayor of Victoria said a few inspiring words before the official opening. In an elegant speech, she focused on gratitude for the hard work that many individuals had put into making the new bridge a reality. The speech was short, effective, and full of positivity. I was grateful to learn from a master.

The afternoon passed with more work on my own presentation. The topic was a previous habitat enhancement project I had completed back in Vancouver. The work was followed by a nap in an armchair positioned perfectly in the sunlight that flooded through one of the tall Juliette windows. It was heavenly. A little before five I called it a day and gathered my things before heading out for dinner at Jenn's.

It took longer than usual to leave downtown because of the heavy long weekend traffic. I spent what seemed like several cycles of lights at the corner of Government and Douglas. Traffic in Victoria typically moved at a snail's pace, but even this was getting absurd. Inching closer to the front, I noticed a young homeless man holding a cardboard sign that read: "Homeless. Money for food. Happy Easter." My heart melted. I looked at him until he returned my gaze. He walked slowly along the grass median to my open window. When he was close enough, I could see the tears in his eyes. I could only imagine how hard it was for him to be out there, begging for money. I handed over a one-dollar coin, the only change I could find in the truck. As I passed it to him, I asked, "What's your story, brother?"

"It's a long one," he said.

"Talk quick, my man," I said, glancing at the traffic lights ahead.

"My girlfriend took our kid. Then all my money. I can't find work."

"Do you have somewhere to sleep?"

"Sort of. The shelters changed the rules. You have to be first-in to get a bed."

The light changed and I reluctantly started to inch forward. "This is your rock bottom man. You will only go up from here. Trust me," I said, gazing deep into his sad eyes before slowly pulling away.

"Thank you," he whispered. I could feel his sincerity. It landed heavy in my heart.

As I drove away, tears started to form in my eyes, the first in over a month. I sensed his *thank you* wasn't just for the money, but also for the brief connection that was made. We were in different places in life—he was homeless, and I was living in a hotel and driving an expensive truck, financially, we couldn't have been further apart—yet we had both felt pain, loss, helplessness. We had both had our darkest moments, but he was only starting his journey into the light. I felt so badly for him, knowing the mountain of challenges he was yet to face.

Farther down the road my emotions took over, as I remembered that I had over one hundred dollars in cash in the backseat. I was disappointed in myself for not thinking quicker—for not being able to help him more. As my tears eventually subsided, I thought more about our fleeting exchange. Even though I had barely helped him financially, I knew my words had had a positive impact.

I wondered, was this my purpose, my passion—to connect deeply with others to help, support and inspire them? It was so simple, yet it was so obvious. It was probably something that many others had already figured out. But I had to experience my dark night of the soul to learn that life wasn't all about helping myself, it was about helping others. Despite the lengthy journey I took to get to that realization, I was grateful to finally understand the lesson. From that moment going forward I would use my words and my voice to leave people better than I found them. I had found my mission, found my purpose, found the one way I could use my gifts to serve others. I had found my dharma.

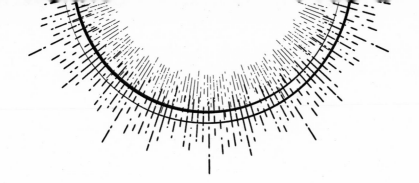

CHAPTER 11

DREAM LIFE

*The future belongs to those who believe
in the beauty of their dreams.*

ELEANOR ROOSEVELT

On Tuesday morning, I woke up in the suite after a decent sleep. I made an espresso and checked emails on my phone. "I'm so sorry, Mike, I'm just too busy to write your book." My heart sank as I read the email from Seb. It had taken her a while to respond to my request for help with my book. I had put a lot of hope in her agreeing to the project. I had already envisioned flying across the world to visit her in Germany to get the book started. In my mind we were already meeting daily at trendy cafés, sipping espressos, while I explained the contents of my journals and she turned it into a book. Now that dream was dead because she had a life of her own—which I of course respected. I could always say I had at least tried to tell my story. But something didn't feel right. It felt wrong not to share the lessons from all that I was learning, about how I was working to turn my nightmare into a dream. Especially since I had just got clear that it was my mission to use my words to help empower others. A powerful story left untold didn't seem like a worthy ending.

The news sat heavy with me as I made my way to Seattle by float plane for the conference. The day had started with so much promise but ended in a lonely hotel room. After weeks of eluding the darkness, my old unwanted companion had crept back in. I had fallen into the trap of creating unrealistic expectations, only to be faced with disappointment. It had happened with Seb and the book, and now it was happening on my first night in a new city. I had assumed that a major conference in a new city would lead to an exciting first night out on the town with new connections. Instead, I had checked in at the conference, then quickly returned to my room. For the first time in over a month I was lonely.

Brittany must have telepathically sensed that I was in a funk. Out of nowhere she texted me a link to a recent podcast interview she had given. In the interview, Brittany beamed as she talked with great confidence about how she helped change her clients' lives. Her coaching usually started by helping her clients eliminate their victim mindset. Often her clients were just coming out of a challenging breakup, job loss, or other setback. In those scenarios her clients would blame their partner or their employer for the pain and suffering they were experiencing. Brittany helped her clients eliminate that mindset by having them take full ownership for all aspects of their lives: their job, their bank account, their health, their looks, and their happiness. For me, my pain had been obvious, with the separation. For months I had let that external event dictate my life. That was the first thing she had helped me overcome. It was a powerful mindset shift.

After victim mindset, the next emotion to overcome was negativity. In the interview she said that a world comprised of negative people, news, thoughts, habits, and feelings, resulted in a negative life. To achieve positivity and happiness, all negativity must be eliminated. "It's a simple concept, but one that many struggle with," she said. For me, I had become obsessed over the previous months by removing myself from any negative situations. If I found myself in a conversation full of negativity and complaints, I'd leave. If I was reading an article that was full of negativity, I'd close it. Remembering that I was in Seattle, I recalled that I couldn't remember the last time I had heard the often-negative voice of America's president. I had consciously eliminated TV from my life and all the noise and advertisements that went with it. By removing the distractions and the negativity, I had created more space for peace and positivity.

Brittany went on to talk about one of the biggest things she worked on with her clients: mental discipline. "Just like muscles in our arms and legs, the brain is a muscle that needs to be exercised. Mental discipline can be learned: discipline to exercise, to eat better, to work harder, to improve time management, to improve every aspect of one's life. Once you master mental discipline, you master your life, and you become unstoppable," she said. Her words were intoxicating. She clearly articulated the syllables of each word, so they landed with authority in the listener's ears.

I had never fully appreciated the concept of mental discipline before I had started working with Brittany. Now I was obsessed. In theory, I had practiced mental discipline throughout my history of endurance sports. I also assumed it was an element of mental discipline that had got me through two engineering degrees. But I never had the appreciation that I could apply that discipline to other aspects of my life to improve my overall happiness.

Brittany moved on to talk about how grateful she was for hitting her rock bottom. For her, it was a rough childhood of extreme bullying that later turned into an adolescence of online bullying. The bullying devastated her life every single day. "At a certain point I said screw it, no more, and I started to take ownership of my life," she said. After that point she focused on reclaiming her self-worth and not letting the opinions of others dictate her life. She used the hateful words by the bullies as motivation to create a better life for herself.

For me, my low point was obvious. As a guy with a big heart, the devastation from the separation was a level of pain I'd never felt before and never wanted to feel again. But I had made a commitment to myself to rebuild and do everything possible to never feel that level of anguish again. I also had a second factor motivating me towards self-improvement. Through the separation it become obvious that there were parts of my old personality that I didn't love. More than the pain of the heartbreak, it was the desire to improve these shortcomings that fueled my fire to evolve. Just like Brittany, I had progressed to switch my mindset and was now grateful for my heartbreak, taking ownership to create a better life for myself.

The interview ended with Brittany reinforcing the importance of clearly defined goals to help guide a structured life of purpose. Her energy and positivity were contagious. Just like during our calls, I immediately felt a renewed sense of optimism.

The conference opening was held the next morning at the Washington State Convention Center. The conference featured the latest scientific research and management issues related to the health of the Salish Sea (the body of water between Vancouver, Victoria, and Seattle) ecosystem. Former Secretary of the Interior, Sally Jewell, gave a passionate speech about protecting our environment and the importance of partnership with Indigenous people. After her speech, I felt pulled to learn more about the social issues surrounding Indigenous people, and less towards the other technical sessions at the conference. I spent the first day attending as many Indigenous themed sessions as possible. I learned that before colonization, the Indigenous people had lived in the Pacific Northwest for thousands of years in harmony with the environment. It appeared we still had much to learn from them.

I did my presentation the following day. I started with gratitude by thanking the organizers and those in attendance for the opportunity to present my project. On an impulse, I added how impressed I was at the high level of government that had opened the conference. "I challenge everyone listening here today to ensure that similar levels of Canadian government are present in two years' time when the conference is held in Vancouver," I said, to the fifty or so people in the room. I was expecting to be floored with thundering applause; instead, silence.

Just like earlier in the week, I still had to work on managing my expectations. While I had already claimed that I wanted to impact people from the stage, I had yet to appreciate the skills that would be required to do so. There was a large gap between where I was and where I wanted to be. It was one thing to say I wanted to command the audience; it was another thing to actually do it. My audacious dreams were exciting in their scope, but I would have to learn to be patient while I grew the skills and faced the fears that separated me from my lofty goals.

Following the morning session on Friday, I made my way to the float plane terminal for the return flight to Victoria. After landing, I went directly to the work site to relieve the co-worker that had been filling in for me. The crew had made good progress while I was away. Our hole was slowly getting filled.

The next day, Saturday, I found myself tired after a long week. After a morning on the work site, I was drained by the afternoon. Knowing how much energy was required, I was in no mood for a scheduled coaching call with Brittany.

"Hello, Michael!" she said, answering my call after the second ring. Despite my initial preference of being called Mike, she had continued to call me Michael since our first call. After some initial resistance, I had decided to roll with it. I figured that perhaps a new name could be part of the new me. Afterall, my mom called me Michael, my boss called me Michael, and now Brittany was calling me Michael; perhaps it was time I started listening to the strong women in my life. Just like I had been shedding other parts of my old world that no longer served me, in that moment, I decided that going forward, I would start using my full name.

Our hour-long calls had taken on a new dynamic since Brittany started losing her voice a couple weeks earlier. After skipping a couple weeks of calls, she suggested that we go ahead with me talking and her replying by text. I was more than skeptical at first, but the format proved to be effective. Following her initial hello, she remained silent for the rest of our call.

I started my update by telling her about the night I quit drinking and how I finally realized I could not afford to waste any more time. After I finished talking, I let the silence hang in the air before a barrage of texts flooded my phone. "That story gave me goosebumps," she wrote, "You absolutely reek with confidence in your decision."

"Thank you," I said, to the silent phone.

"What do you want your legacy to be?" she texted. "How do you want to be remembered?" Just as I did when she first asked about my goals, I struggled to answer to the question.

"Well, I guess I'd like people to smile when they thought of me, to feel good at my memory, and to help them feel better in some way."

"Bullshit, what do you really want?" she texted.

I took a deep breath as I read her message—she knew me better than I knew myself. She knew when I was playing small. She could read me so well: it was both infuriating and intoxicating. I took another deep breath and replied, "I guess I want to change the world."

"YES."

"I want to make a difference."

"YES."

"I want to make a huge difference."

"YES. That's what I'm talking about."

Silence lingered in the air after the intense exchange. We moved on to talk about time management and how to consciously recognize how my time was being spent. She challenged me to be aware of when I was wasting time and procrastinating. She gave me three simple reminders to ask myself obsessively throughout the day: what was I doing in that moment, what was I thinking, and where was I? If any of the answers to those questions were not in alignment with me continuing to evolve and achieve my goals, then I was tasked with immediately changing what I was doing or thinking or getting into a more inspiring location.

We moved on to talk about my resistance to telling my story. I told her how, in Seattle, I had held back telling people about what I had been through, about how I was transforming.

"You've transformed?" she texted.

"Yes, of course I have, where have you been?" I asked, perplexed.

"LOL, only kidding."

She had made her point. I was missing out on more meaningful conversations because I was holding back. I was letting opportunities for real connections pass by. I wasn't inspiring others by keeping my story to myself.

"Alright, I'll lean into it. I'm up for a challenge. I'll start sharing even more about what I've been going through," I said, even though I was still having trouble fully articulating exactly what it was I had been through.

Just as we were about to end the call, she broke her self-imposed silence and said, "I'm sorry, but can I interrupt you?" I was fearing the worst, bracing for more uncomfortable homework, or the revealing of something obvious I had missed.

"Um, ya. Okay."

"Can I just say how proud I am of you. How far you've come in such a short period of time. Your progress is amazing. It's like nothing I've ever seen before. You talk different, you sound different, your confidence is growing daily. You are becoming a new version of you. You are becoming a new Michael."

Or a new Mike, perhaps? I kept the thought to myself. I was too exhausted to share my wit.

"Thank you. I could not have done it without you," I said, instead.

The next time I heard from Brittany was a few days later, on Tuesday morning. As I was getting ready for work, her texts started bombarding my phone: she could text faster than most people could speak. As the texts came in, I tried to take notes, but it was hard to keep up. She was feeding me information on raising the quality of my social media posts. She had been encouraging me to continue sharing my thoughts online. She even challenged me to be more vulnerable and share even more about my struggles. It had started as an exercise to help build my confidence, but it seemed to be shifting into something more.

Soon we were messaging about strategies to grow my following and build a loyal audience. I was unclear exactly what I was building an audience for, but I trusted her. It was as though she could see several steps ahead of what I saw. I was still resistant to the idea of me becoming a coach, but she seemed to have an idea of where I was headed, and I was doing my best to hang on. She said I needed to fill my posts with value and have one big idea that was different than anyone else.

"When you build your value alongside your unique perspective, your audience will grow. You must write your posts for your audience, not for yourself. Focus on their needs, not your own. You must get into their heads, you must answer the questions that you know they have, and you must engage with your followers. That is the key to help grow your following," she texted.

"Alright, I'm on it," I replied.

"Oh, and you should think about getting a photo shoot—it's the best way to get high quality images."

"A photoshoot? I've never done that before." Even though I had had the vision a few weeks ago, it was another thing to talk about getting it done.

"Yeah, a photoshoot. You'll love it!"

"Alright, whatever you say."

"I love it."

"Oh, hey, I've been looking for a book to help explain, um, you know, all these changes that have been going on in my mind. I need to better understand what I've been through. I've tried a few books, but they're just not doing it. Got anything to recommend?" I asked.

"Dr. Joe."

"Dr. Joe?"

"Dr. Joe. Joe Dispenza. He's your man."

"Epic. I'll check him out."

"I love it. I love your world-class mindset and your pursuit of excellence in every aspect of your life. Now let's kick it to the next level!"

Fired up, I grabbed my gear and sprang out of the suite headed for work. As I was walking the short distance from the hotel to the truck, my phone vibrated with another incoming message. It was Anne. "What are you doing Saturday, April 21st?" she texted.

"Um, no plans," I replied.

"Do you want to go to a cocktail party at the Vancouver Club?"

The Vancouver Club was one of Vancouver's premier private clubs. I'd been wanting to go there for years. Anne was a gorgeous girl and we seemed to get along fine over text, but I hadn't met her in person. Plus, it had been well over a decade since I had been on a date. I was hesitant to commit, but I was also fired up from the morning texts with Brittany.

"Sure, why not!"

"Awesome!"

New Michael had arrived.

———————

After work I went directly to the bookstore. I started my search for Dr. Joe in the self-help section. Walking through the section I realized it was the biggest in the store, taking up half the bottom floor. I wondered why the section was so big. Were there that many people looking for help? Were there that many people looking for more passion, purpose, and fulfillment from life?

With help from a clerk, I found my guy, Dr. Joe. I picked up one of his books, *Evolve Your Brain*[9], and started to read through his biography. Ever since he had healed his broken back through the power of thought, he had dedicated his life's work to better understanding the brain and the connection to the mind. I scanned through a few pages of the book and learned that thoughts create chemical reactions. These chemical reactions keep you addicted to habitual feelings and patterns—including feeling unhappy. Once you knew how these bad habits were created, you could learn how to break them. Not only that, but once you learned how to break the bad habits, you could rewire your brain so that positive habits could take over.

The book seemed to validate some of the changes I had experienced over the last few months. I had started to shift my thoughts and feelings out of the darkness that lingered after the separation. My challenge was that I knew a change was taking place, but I still couldn't explain how it was happening. As a stubborn engineer, I preferred to know how things worked. My hope was that, with Dr. Joe's book, I could better understand what I had been through, so I could help others move out of their darkness.

Before leaving the bookstore, I also picked up Dr. Joe's latest book: *Becoming Supernatural*[10]. The book described how common people

---

9 Dispenza, Joe. *Evolve Your Brain: The Science of Changing Your Mind.*
Health Communications Inc., 2008.

10 Dispenza, Joe. *Becoming Supernatural: How Common People are Doing the Uncommon.*
Hay House Inc, 2017.

were doing the uncommon to transform themselves and their lives. That sounded epic to me. After paying for the books, I made my way out of the store. Walking onto the street I had a thought: if I could gain a better understanding of what I had been through, there was no reason why I couldn't continue my transformation and also become supernatural. It was invigorating to consider, but all this *transformation* talk was still so new. Thoughts creating chemical reactions and people rewiring their brains to becoming supernatural; I had a lot to learn, but I was hungry to do so. Once I arrived back at the suite, I spent a of couple hours digging into the new books.

With my last ounce of energy before bed, I loaded David Ji's "Manifesting Your Dreams" meditation on my phone. Against a background of soothing music, Ji repeated that thoughts are electrical energy, and our feelings are magnetic energy. When we think and feel a vision of our dreams at the same time, we can attract them to manifest in our lives. Ji added that the heart is the most important vehicle for creation because it can generate the highest feeling of gratitude, which is vital for creation. By elevating our emotions to a feeling of gratitude, and holding a vision of our dreams, we can manifest the reality that is our dream lives. My mind was blown. I had to master this. But first, I had to get crystal clear on what exactly I wanted in my dream life.

More delays were experienced on-site the next day. During the backfilling of our hole, the levels of suspended sediment in the ocean had exceeded environmental limits. To allow the water quality time to improve, site work was cancelled for the remainder of day and all the next day. Every delay was pushing us against our targeted completion date of the end of April. With each setback everyone involved on the project—the owner, the contractor, the consultants—became more anxious. I wasn't overly concerned, especially since the time off corresponded with an incoming wave swell out on the coast.

The next morning, I was up early and out the door before seven. I was eager to make the hour-and-a-half drive out to the coast to catch some waves. I spent a couple hours in the water on both my surfboard and paddleboard. The cold water served to accentuate the connection with nature, even through my thick wetsuit. After the session, I stopped in at a rustic seaside café for an early lunch. I ordered a sandwich and coffee, then took a seat outside in the sun. Since it was midweek, I was the only one sitting on the gravel patio. The April sun cut through the tall Douglas-fir, Sitka spruce and Western red-cedar trees that surrounded the café. The roar of the nearby ocean could be heard as I settled my tired muscles into an Adirondack chair. My bare feet rested below me, connected to the earth.

As I waited for the food to arrive, I caught up on emails on my phone. In one of the emails, I finalized the arrangements to have a co-worker take over for me should the project extend into May. I had been holding off booking my travel plans for the month of May, but now that I had a backup in place, it was time to commit.

Since early March I had been thinking about joining my sister and her family in Nicaragua on their upcoming trip in May. They had purchased the property a year earlier and extended an open invite to all family members. I was coming to the end of my time in Victoria, and I was in no rush to get back to my old life in Vancouver. I had never been to Central America, but it felt like the time was right to explore.

As I sat basking in the sun, I booked the first week of my trip to start at a surf camp in northwestern Nicaragua. Next, I made the trip official by booking a flight. I wasn't clear on how long I would stay and where I would return to, so I just booked a one-way ticket. I had never had such open-ended plans, but again, it felt right.

Lunch was delivered to me on the patio. As I enjoyed the sandwich, I pulled my journal from my bag to record a few thoughts about my upcoming trip. I wanted to make sure the trip was purposeful—I didn't do well just lying on beaches all day. I made a list of the goals for my upcoming adventure: I wanted to be sure to connect with new people and make new friends; I wanted to explore new places to help awaken new connections in my brain—just like I had been doing in Victoria; I wanted to experience new cultures through music and art; I wanted to use the time away to continue to learn more about myself and get further in touch with my deepest desires; I wanted to read, I wanted to write, I wanted to meditate in the jungle, I wanted to surf in the warm ocean; I wanted to get further clarity on my purpose, and lastly, I wanted to maintain an element of productivity. I still wasn't sure what exactly I would be working on, but I had set the intention, and was confident that clarity would emerge. Satisfied with my list, I reached again into my bag and pulled out my new companion, Dr. Joe.

A few pages in, I learned how evolution begins with changing oneself: when one member of a pack decides to go against the grain and break free from the behaviour of the others. This rogue must have the intuition to act in new ways and break free. At a high level, this rebellion could be the only way to ensure the survival of a group. The rogue often leaves behind what is considered normal to society and instead creates a new normal or a new mindset to ensure the survival of his kin.

I felt, to an extent, like I was this rogue. Since the separation I had put distance between myself and certain friends, family, and really, my old self. In the beginning, I had been so fixated on better understanding of what had led to the separation in the first place. To get that better understanding, I needed that distance to focus on myself. As my self-awareness muscle grew, it slowly led to a deeper desire to better understand who I was. I had to break free of old environments and old thought patterns as I attempted to go deeper within. I started to become more mindful of how I could better control my thoughts while moving forward in a positive direction. In doing so, I became obsessed with filling the cleared space in my mind with empowering thoughts, a positive outlook, and uninhibited optimism. I had changed my outlook, my perspective, on so many aspects of my world. I was teaching myself how to see opportunities in challenging situations.

I had been thrust into my low point, but somehow while I was down there, I had begun to face and transform all the unsavoury bits of my soul that I didn't want to carry forward. As an engineer, I knew in order to rebuild the strongest version of myself, I had to re-establish a rock-solid foundation. It was as though my life was a mirror to the work we were doing on-site: I had dredged many of the contaminated thoughts from my mind and started to replace them with clean material. That process was something I was ready to share with my tribe.

I read on and learned that the brain possesses elasticity and it's not hardwired as many scientists previously thought. Instead, it can be rewired through the simple act of having new experiences. New experiences create new thoughts, which create new chemicals, which create a new brain. Dr. Joe was validating what I had lived. My new experiences had started way back in November, with that first night out at Barney's. Although it was in the same neighbourhood I had lived in for years, the experience of dining alone, of connecting with strangers, of really listening to what my new friends were feeling—it was all so new to me. The new experiences had continued since I had been in Victoria. As I had learned to fully embrace my new circumstances, I could only assume that I too had created new chemicals, and a new brain. I thought ahead in excitement to my upcoming travels and all the new experiences I was sure to have. My trip was going to fuel further evolution.

I took a break from reading and sat in silence. The sun continued to warm my skin, which was still salty from the morning surf. The air was pure and fresh, having traveled thousands of miles across the empty Pacific. The giant trees swayed nearby in a rhythmic dance. I sat connected to it all.

I was outside, I was learning, I was thinking, I was enjoying good food, I was sore from exercise, I was being productive, and I was doing it all on my terms. I was in the zone, in a state of flow. I had always believed that I had to be sitting behind a desk to be productive. I had also bought into the program that the only way to get better results was to push harder. Sitting barefoot amongst nature, I was getting a glimpse into a different model of living and working. I reached for my phone to share the moment.

"This is it sis; I'm finally living the dream, my dream," I texted my sister, Jane.

"Amazing! You Go Mikey!" She replied.

The moment was fleeting, but it was profound. I had spent years sarcastically saying that I was 'living the dream' when it was a lie. I usually found myself sarcastically saying the line while at work sitting in an office behind a computer. That was not my dream life; instead, it was a lie I had been telling myself for years. I knew I couldn't sit on the heavenly oceanside chair forever, but in that moment, I had felt what it meant to be fully in the zone, fully present, living *my* dream. I was getting clearer on what I wanted in my future. I was learning to control my mind to create the life of my dreams. I had felt the feeling; next I had to learn how to prolong the fleeting moment. I also had to continue to get clear on what else I wanted to pull into my future. I was determined to let the new me, the new Michael, live his dream life.

———————

Construction resumed Friday on the work site. Good progress was made on both Friday and Saturday. Saturday night came around and I was content to spend it alone, reading in the hotel suite. It had only been a couple of weeks since I stopped drinking, but I was already noticing changes. My energy was up, my mind was clearer, and I had even started to lose weight from the soft layer that had always hung around my waist. I hadn't experienced any cravings at all. I wondered why I didn't give it up earlier.

Another totally unexpected change had occurred, something I had not anticipated at all. For the first time since I could remember, I noticed how long my fingernails were getting. My nails had always grown, but unconsciously I had been biting them for years. I couldn't even remember the last time I had used nail clippers. But ever since I quit drinking, I couldn't even bring myself to consider biting my nails—the very thought suddenly was disgusting. It was the strangest thing: by removing the poisonous alcohol from my body, the signal that had triggered my brain to bite my nails had gone off. It was incredible.

While it had been relatively easy to leave alcohol behind, I had a new challenge on my hands. As the evening wore on, the noise from the bar below grew to a dull roar. The few guests that had visited the suite had all commented that it would drive them mad. Well I didn't mind the noise as much from the bar below, it was the noise from the traffic outside the thin windows that was starting to wear on me. The sharp, high-pitched whine of passing cars and trucks was not soothing my soul. I reminded myself that I only had to endure the noise for a few more weeks before I took off on my trip.

For the most part, I had adapted to the bar noise by wearing earplugs. I put them in as I took a seat on the living room sofa with my journal. My intention was to get further clarity on what exactly my dream life looked like. I had been learning to work with the Universe, I was learning to manifest my dreams. I had had some success already with the backstage concert experience. My recent time out on the coast had given me clarity on what it felt like to be in a flow state, fully in the moment. I was learning from Dr. Joe and David Ji about the relationship between energy, thoughts, and emotions. I felt that if I kept going, I would be able to manifest all I desired. The question was, what did I truly desire?

If it was that easy, why not choose a life of luxury: jets, yachts, and mansions? I wondered if that was what I really wanted. I mean, who could say no to luxury? At the same time, I felt there had to be more; not more things, but more impact, more meaning, more purpose to my dream life. Thinking back, I remembered that since the separation I had made a conscious effort to get rid of as many physical things as possible. Back in the condo in Vancouver, I had cleared drawers down to empty, donated extra clothes and sold unused bikes. It was a complete rinsing of as many material items as possible. It felt so good in my brain. It was as though, by becoming a minimalist, I was freeing space in my mind to achieve further clarity on who I was and all I desired. For that reason, it didn't make sense to dream about accumulating more things.

Plus, it didn't seem to be in alignment with my dharma, my mission, my purpose, to help and inspire others using my words and my voice.

My dream life had to be something more. I thought again to my time on the coast a few days earlier. I had been so in the moment, so peaceful when I was writing in my journal. When I was writing I had become one with the words, one with the nature around me, one with the thoughts I was placing on the page. Writing was still so new to me—it had been less than six months since I had first opened a blank journal after the breakup. At that time there were so many thoughts swirling through my mind. I used the journal as a place to store them. The act of writing by hand on paper seemed to slow the racing thoughts down and help me process what was happening. Since those early days I had journaled my thoughts on a daily basis. It had been so therapeutic to get the confusion out of my head.

In my growing volume of journals, I was accumulating a record of all that had transpired since the separation. It had been my original vision that I would hand these journals off to Seb and she would transform them into a book. Since she had said she was too busy to take on the project, that was no longer an option.

The music from the bar below started pounding at a higher volume interrupting my train of thought. It was getting near the time of night when the dance floor came to life. There was only a thin cover of original hardwood separating me from the madness below. I pushed my ear plugs in further to block out the noise.

Then I had a new thought. If I was learning how to create my dream life, then why couldn't I create a life where I wrote the book myself? If I had the power within me to manifest all I desired, then why wouldn't I just learn how to write? I knew a shift had happened within me, and I knew it was for the better. I also knew that I still couldn't fully understand or explain the changes that were occurring. But I did know that I was learning skills that could benefit others. While I was still learning how to clearly articulate exactly what those teachings were, I knew with time I could make sense of it all. The thought of writing the book myself felt good, it felt right. That feeling matched that same feeling of bliss I had felt out on the coast. I had the feeling, and I was beginning to see the vision of how I could write my story.

Brittany had helped me see that I wanted to make a big impact. So, if I was going to write a book, I wanted to write a great book. If I was going to manifest myself into an author and write a book, then why not make it a bestseller? Heck, if I was dreaming big, then why not one day watch my story on the big screen as a Hollywood movie?

My dream life was starting to feel good. But I didn't want to live the dream alone. I wanted a wife, I wanted kids, I wanted a family of my own. I wanted a life full of love, connection, meaningful conversations, and incredible relationships with family and friends. I wanted to travel, to eat the best food, see the best views, hear the best sounds, have the best sex, laugh endlessly, continue to learn, and speak on the world's biggest stages. I wanted it all.

I remembered Dr. Joe's instructions to match the clarity of my thoughts with the elevated emotions I would experience when my dream life manifested. When all of those dreams came true I would feel joy, I would feel gratitude, I would feel love, I would feel freedom, I would feel like I was living on purpose, living with passion, living like I was connected with everyone and everything around me. I would feel peace. I knew from Dr. Joe's teachings that the key to manifesting one's dream life was not to wait for my dreams to become a reality before feeling these emotions, rather it was other way around: to feel these emotions in the present moment, to attract my dream life to me.

I closed my journal and started getting ready for bed. Once in bed I fell asleep quickly. The music was blaring right below my bed, but in my mind, I was in a faraway place already living my dream life.

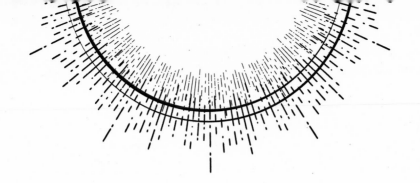

CHAPTER 12

FACING FEAR

The cave you fear to enter
holds the treasure you seek.

JOSEPH CAMPBELL

took my next call with Brittany on Monday during lunch break on-site. She was still resting her voice, so again I spoke while she coached me by text. I walked around one of the unused barges as I gave her my update. Walking and talking had become a new habit for me. I had learned it from the site superintendent, who was always on his phone pacing around our floating site. It was a combination of two simple actions—walking and talking—but for some reason the physical movement helped me focus on a deeper level.

"I've been good. My productivity is up since I quit drinking, I feel positive, and I'm getting more and more clear on the new life I want to create," I reported to Brittany. "But sometimes, I don't know, I certainly wouldn't say I'm one hundred percent confident. All these changes I'm making, and all these new goals I'm setting, sometimes fear sets in and I start to doubt myself."

"Do you know why that happens?" she texted.

It was annoyingly endearing when she asked that question. "No, Brittany, I do not."

"Because your mind wavers, you have a moment of weakness. You get scared of venturing into the unknown. It is easier to waver, but it takes courage to be strong, and this new Michael is a warrior. He is a champion that dominates his goals. These moments of doubt will become less as you become stronger and grow into the person you want to be. Confidence is key to facing your fears and moving into the unknown. Strengthening your confidence in yourself is key to becoming who you want to be. You have grown already: you speak differently, you are clearer and more confident, and that is exactly what other people want to be around. Why? Because people want to be led, so lead them. Be a leader. Speak out about your awakening and transformation. You are more powerful than you know. I hope that really sits with you. I hope you really hear that."

I remained silent as the last of the texts bombarded my phone. I was still in awe at the speed and volume of her texts; the energy transferred was astounding.

"I also want you to become a laser-focused excuse detective. Keep an eye out for where you are making up excuses that are holding you back from facing your fears. When you become an expert at identifying excuses as they appear, it becomes easier to knock them down and move forward towards your goals."

"Okay, I'm on it."

"That's what I like to hear. You are becoming a machine, Michael. You can create anything you put your mind to. I want you to focus hard on pursuing excellence in every aspect of your life, because the way you do anything, is the way you do everything."

I had heard the quote before, but I couldn't place it. Either way, the words were powerful. I always felt energized after our calls and that call was no exception. I felt fired-up throughout the rest of the workday.

With thoughts of pursuing excellence in my mind, I stopped by a suit store on my way home from work. I had decided to treat myself to a new suit, since I had committed to attending the cocktail party in Vancouver with Anne. Once inside the store, a clerk helped me try on a few different styles. "Hot damn, that is the one!" she said, as I tried on the third suit she had brought out. The suit was a light blue Strellson that fit like perfection. It had been over fifteen years since I'd had a new suit. I felt like a million bucks inside the quality fabric. "I don't disagree. I'll take it," I said.

After I paid for the suit, I made my way back to the suite to finish a few remaining work tasks. Once I was done, I collapsed onto the living room couch. The suite always had a great energy, but it seemed extra magic during the quieter weeknights. It was named after the former hotel owner, also named Michael. He had been a popular community philanthropist, visionary and art collector. His collection was hung throughout the hotel, including several pieces in my suite. I could feel his stately presence each time I looked at the art.

Sitting on the couch, I opened my laptop and loaded a Dr. Joe video I had been wanting to watch. The video started with a review of the three brains that made up our larger brain: the neocortex, the limbic, and the cerebellum. These brains were often referred to as the 'thinking', the 'doing', and the 'being' brains. The three brains worked together to form who we are. The video focused on the newest portion of our brain, the neocortex.

Dr. Joe repeated that "nerve cells that fire together, wire together," and that when you learn something new or have a new experience, we build new cells in our brain. In watching the video, I learned that to modify our behaviour we need to modify what we are thinking. That works because the body is the unconscious mind and is a direct reflection of what we are thinking. Once we got into a new routine of thinking differently, new nerve cells in our brain would strengthen their connection and the old ones would weaken. That was how we changed who we were: we become aware of the thoughts we want to remove—like negativity, anger, sadness—and we replace them with the elevated emotions of bliss, joy, freedom, happiness, and gratitude. I wondered if I could do the same with all the fear I had been feeling. I wanted to replace thoughts of fear with thoughts of courage.

The whole process was summed up in one word: metacognition, which means: how we observe who we are being, how we think about what we are thinking about, how we pay attention to how we react, and how we notice what we are feeling. By modifying our behaviour, we could become better versions of ourselves and silence the old circuits of our old selves. It sounded easy enough, but as I had already experienced, it was going to take a lot more uncomfortable change to evolve into the new vision I was crafting for myself.

Everything Dr. Joe was saying I had lived, to an extent. I had made the commitment to change my mind away from the pain, sorrow, and sadness. As those thoughts diminished, I made space for elevated emotions to move in. It wasn't a perfect science and I still struggled at times, but I had made progress. It was that little bit of progress that gave me the confidence to believe I could continue to evolve.

The work week passed without any breakdowns or interruptions on-site. We made good progress filling our hole. Friday night I failed miserably trying to get a good sleep before my date in Vancouver with Anne. During the night, I was woken by the sound of loud sex coming from the room next door. In the past that sort of thing would have triggered anger and most likely led to me banging on the wall. But that time was different, and I genuinely felt happy for the couple. I also thought that perhaps it was a sign for what was to come with my night out with Anne. On Saturday morning I was wide awake before the sun was up—my mind racing with excitement.

After a morning run, I made the short walk to the float plane terminal to catch a flight to Vancouver. Once I landed in Vancouver, I caught a taxi to my first stop: a long overdue haircut with Caitie. After I arrived, Caitie got to work on my hair as I filled her in on my plans for the evening. "I'm meeting a woman I met online. We're going out to dinner and then to some fancy party at the Vancouver Club for a TV show she works on," I said.

"Sounds dreamy!" said Caitie.

"I know, eh! I figured it was a good excuse for a new suit and a night in a hotel."

"I love it!"

"Then just yesterday I had the idea to get some photos taken before I met her. My buddy's cousin is just getting started out and he's looking to build his portfolio."

"You're getting a photoshoot done—that's wild!"

"Tell me about it! I've never done anything like this before, but I thought if I was going to get all dressed up, I might as well."

"You should stop by Sephora to get your makeup done."

"Um, what? Me? Makeup? I don't think so."

"Yeah, they'll do it for free! They'll just do a quick touch-up. You'll love it!"

I was already feeling fear with the suit, the hotel, and first date in what seemed like forever. The thought of adding to my fear—with a makeup session—made me even more uncomfortable. But I knew if I wanted to step into my dream life, I was going to have to continue to rewire my mind from what was holding me back.

"Alright, if you say so."

"You are kind of turning into a new dude, eh?"

"Yes, I suppose I am."

Following the haircut, I walked a few blocks through downtown to Sephora. The makeup artist was able to fit me in right away and only took a few minutes to smooth out the redness across my face. Once we were done, I crossed the street to the hotel and checked in. I made my way to the room and started to change into my new suit. As I was getting dressed, I thought back to my request to the Universe a few weeks earlier for backstage passes, something new and amazing to wear, and a photoshoot with an aspiring young photographer. The backstage experience had happened back in March with Jake, now the other two parts of my vision were coming to reality. I was learning how to make my visions come true. A knock on the door interrupted my thoughts. It was Ryan, the photographer.

I was only half-dressed, wearing pants and no shirt, when I answered the door. "Ah don't worry man, it's not that kind of shoot," I said, letting him in and breaking the ice. Ryan made his way into the room and started getting set up. Before I got fully dressed, I asked him to get a few shots of my latest piece of art: a new tattoo.

The night before, I had returned to the studio on Government Street to get the words, "helping is transcendence," written in cursive, across my left inner bicep. The phrase was another tribute to my fallen hero, Gord Downie. The lyric was from a song, "Spoon", off his final solo album. In the song, Gord described a trip he took to Maui with his daughter. On the trip, his daughter taught him that he could help heal her broken leg, simply by walking the beach with her each day. She taught Gord, her father, that helping her and helping others, was above anything else that mattered in this world.

I chose the phrase to make a commitment to my new direction in life: my passion, my purpose, my dharma, to help others through my words and my voice. I also got the tattoo to mark the beginning of another chapter in my life: coaching. Like most things Brittany had suggested, it had taken a few weeks for me to come around and see how I too could be a coach. It felt right; I was living through my own transformation, I was already impacting people by sharing what I was learning, and to some extent, I felt like it was my responsibility. Since I had made progress out of my darkness, I had knowledge that could help others do the same. If it was possible to serve others, then it felt right to do so.

After Ryan got a few shots of the tattoo, I finished getting dressed. Once I was dressed, we made our way to the elevators. On the ride down I explained who I was and how the photos would be used for social media and a future website. "I'm writing my transformational story and launching a coaching business," I said. It felt great, but it was also scary to speak those words into existence.

"That's awesome, dude!" said Ryan, as we reached the lobby.

It didn't take long for Ryan and me to find our groove. Once outside, he directed me to walk north on the sidewalk opposite the hotel, while he shot from across the street. Ryan wasn't satisfied with the lighting, so we headed a half block south, to the Vancouver Art Gallery. After a few shots on the grand staircase, we continued another half-block south, to a secluded terrace in front of the law courts. The whole experience was so new to me, so I took every cue from Ryan to get the best shots possible.

I was in unfamiliar territory. I was wearing an amazing suit getting photographed walking around downtown Vancouver in the middle of the day. As uncomfortable as I was, it felt right to be in the spotlight: subconsciously, that was where I'd always wanted to be. The problem was it had always come from a place of ego, a desire that was only serving myself. Now I had reason beyond myself to start building a personal brand, I had a mission to serve others. "You look like a boss!" Ryan said, between shots.

Once we had enough photographs, we made our way back towards the entrance to the art gallery. It was time for my rendezvous with Anne. At first, I couldn't see her amongst the crowd. We had exchanged a few photos by text, but I began to wonder if I would be able to recognize her in person. Eventually I did see her—she was not hard to miss: a stunning blonde wearing two-inch heels, a floor-length orange dress, and a matching cardigan—she looked incredible.

As she approached, she reached out to nervously shake my hand. Instead, I grabbed her hand and pulled her in for a hug. We had been messaging for about a month, so it felt good to connect in person after the deep conversations we had had. Despite the sunny skies, she was cold. We bid Ryan goodbye and headed back towards the hotel.

I held her tightly as we crossed Georgia Street. When we reached the other side of the street, she stopped me and moved in for a long and passionate kiss. Time stood still as I tasted her lips and ran my hand through her long hair. The passing crowd blurred into nothingness. It had been so long since I had felt a woman's touch. It was going to be a great night.

Half a block later we arrived at the hotel lobby. We spent some time on the couch so she could warm up. It was great to talk in person after so much texting. It was also great to feel that hot desire again, I wanted her right then and there.

More than a few heads turned an hour later as I led her to our table at the restaurant. "No, no, you sit over here, beside me," she said, motioning to her side of the table as we sat down. I loved how forward she was, confident in what she wanted. After we took our seats, she removed her cardigan to reveal the fit body of a former professional athlete. The restaurant was warm, so I removed my jacket and rolled up my shirt sleeves. We managed to sneak in some conversation as we reviewed the menus, but for the most part we were focused on exploring each other's bodies. She had no hesitation to continue kissing between our interactions with our server. As we kissed, she would trace the wave tattoo on my arm or explore the outline of my face. My body came alive with her touch.

During dinner, she told me about her experience with Transcendental Meditation and how she could experience lifelike scenes as she meditated. I was fascinated by her abilities to direct her mind to the visions she wanted to manifest; that was something I wanted to learn more about. I pressed her for as many details as possible, in between sessions of her pressing her lips against mine. We were both happy to indulge the other; neither of us deterred by the others in the restaurant. We slowly made our way through dinner, savouring the taste of the food, and of each other.

"Sorry to interrupt," said our waiter, in the middle of our post-dinner make-out session, "But the next reservation is due to arrive shortly, are you wanting to stay at this table much longer?"

We all laughed. Time had stood still at our table but had continued to tick by for everyone else. "Oh wow, we had no idea how much time had passed," I said, with a grin. "We'd love to stay a little longer if possible." The manager pulled some strings to accommodate our extended date. We eventually made our exit after splurging on dessert.

It was too early to go to the film party, so we stopped by a nearby hotel lounge known for its live blues music. We took a seat in front of the fireplace. I ordered us two hot chocolates, continuing our alcohol-free evening. The kissing and the touching resumed as our drinks arrived. I was at her mercy as she seductively outlined the stubble on my face, before proceeding to suck on my finger. "You're teasing me," I said.

"No, I'm not," she replied, "I'm appreciating you."

"Oh, that's what you call it, eh?"

"Shush, come here," she said, pulling me in for another kiss.

After the kiss ran its course, I asked, "Is there even a party, or did you trick me into coming over for this night out?"

"Of course, there is!"

"Well, that would have been pretty badass of you to trick me."

"I would never do such a thing. We could head over now as the party should be underway. Do you want to go?"

Despite my excitement of rubbing shoulders with the film crowd, I was tired after a long work week and a short sleep the night before. Plus, I was more than content to be the object of a beautiful woman's attention, while listening to live music in the lounge of one of Vancouver's swankiest hotels.

"Not at all, you?" I replied.

"Not one bit," she said, wrapping her hand around the back of my neck and pulling me into her lips.

Pressure started to mount from other patrons eyeing our coveted seats. My internal temperature was also rising from the heat of the fireplace and the relentless heavy petting. When the band took a break a few songs later I announced, "We have to get going soon. I'm melting."

We held each other on the slow walk back to the hotel. I could sense that her soul had also come alive with the physical touch. It had been months since my last kiss with Rebecca. Even then, it was nothing like the passion I was feeling on that night with Anne. I didn't want the night to end. Although I sensed we were walking so slowly because it would be over when we reached the hotel. We arrived at the hotel entrance and I held her tightly under the shimmering marquee lights. I kissed her with everything I had in what I already knew was a futile effort—she was not coming upstairs.

She must have been reading my mind. "Never on the first date, my dear," she said, as she winked at me. "But will I see you again?"

We both knew there wasn't any real long-term hope for us. One of the reasons being that she had made it clear she didn't want kids, while I was consciously creating a future that included them. "Well, I'm heading back to Victoria tomorrow, then I'm off to Central America soon after that. So only time will tell," I said.

We released our embrace and she turned to cross the street to a waiting taxi. After the taxi pulled away, I turned to make my way through the lobby towards the elevators. I exhaled deeply as the elevator lifted me skyward. After a night of fiery embrace, I was alone again. I felt disappointed that she wasn't coming back to the room. But compared to the past, I processed the frustration differently. In the past, my temper would have flared after tallying the cost of the suit, hotel, dinner, twelve-dollar hot chocolates, only to end up with no sex. As the elevator reached my floor, my mind started to drift in that angry direction—but I stopped it; I wouldn't let my thoughts go there. I was deploying the 'awareness muscle' I had been growing. I knew if I let my mind trend in a negative direction it could easily spiral into darkness. I had played that game before with grief; I didn't want to play it again with anger.

Instead, I smiled as I opened the door to the room. I thought about how grateful I was for such a magical day: a beautiful oceanside run in Victoria, an incredible float plane ride to Vancouver, the haircut with Catie, the makeup session, the photoshoot with Ryan, followed by dinner and live music with Anne. That was where I put my focus: on gratitude. Gratitude for an amazing day facing my fears and stepping into the unknown.

By the time I woke up Sunday, the sun was already coming through the hotel windows. My first thoughts of the day were of both excitement and fear. The excitement from the previous day still lingered. I realized the reason the night was so magical was because some of my senses, that had been neglected for so long, were finally reawakened. The touch of Anne's hand tracing my jaw, the taste of her lips against mine, the smell when I buried my head in her soft neck; activation of these senses was what I had been missing. I couldn't even imagine how great sex was going to feel. I had a lot to look forward to.

But it was the fear that weighed heaviest in the back of my mind. Fear that I was making a huge mistake; fear that I was making a fool of myself with photo shoots, talk of writing a book and launching a coaching business. Fear that my dream life would never come to reality. Who was I to write a book, let alone a bestseller? People spent years writing professionally without achieving the level of success that I wanted. It was almost disrespectful to them to assume I could write a bestseller on my first try. I had been writing technical reports for years in engineering, plus I had written a master thesis, but writing a transformational memoir was different—I had no experience in that realm. My thoughts were the same for coaching: who was I to help people? I had been through my own challenges and come out the other side, but real coaches train for years before helping others. Who was I to just dive in?

Still lying in bed, I texted my thoughts to Brittany. She replied instantly: "Fears are False Evidence Appearing Real. They lie. Once you become fearless, you become limitless."

Her words were powerful, but still, it was becoming clear that overcoming fear was going to be a constant challenge for me.

Midway through the following week, the construction schedule was thrown off when the main excavator experienced a major breakdown. The repair would take at least few days to complete and would push the project into May. Since I had already booked my flight to Nicaragua, the delay meant I would not see the project through to completion. It wasn't an ideal scenario, as I had been the main engineer on-site since the start of the project. But it wasn't the end of the world, I had a backup engineer ready to go. The truth was that my heart was no longer in the project. My mind was already focusing on the adventure that lay ahead, and less so with filling an underwater hole.

On Wednesday morning I started the day with a run along the

ocean. The run was followed by breakfast in the hotel suite. As I was eating at the dining room table, I opened my laptop to catch up on emails. I opened one from Ryan that included a few shots from our photoshoot a few days earlier. The pictures were awesome. Ryan nailed capturing the late afternoon lighting on the buildings, the pop of my blue suit, and the optimism in my eyes. I had to share the photos, so I posted a few on social media.

My mom was first to respond, in her typical direct style, "Why can't you just be boring!?" she wrote, half-jokingly. Mom, like many of my friends and family, had been watching my journey from a distance. I had been sharing my thoughts online ever since the separation, and more vulnerably since Brittany had encouraged me to do so. When I first started sharing, my posts would reflect the darkness I had been carrying at the time. I imagined that was hard for everyone to see. Over the previous month or so, I had been sharing more motivating posts along with photos of myself in good spirits. Based on some of the messages I had received from friends, I could tell they were questioning the authenticity of my posts. I sensed some of them thought I was projecting a false happiness. I still had some tough days, but I knew the worst of the pain was behind me. I was stepping into the light, and there were people who would be inspired witnessing that change. It felt good to share and I wasn't going to let others' doubts prevent me from doing so.

I had followed through on the intention I had set months ago: to get closer to knowing my true self while in Victoria. I had become clearer on who I was and what I wanted in life. I had started getting visions of what my best life could look like. I knew I had to chase that life to be fulfilled. I saw glimpses of my full potential through writing a book, speaking on stages, and starting a business. I couldn't fall back to my old, comfortable, safe world, not after I had seen and felt what the future could hold. I was only beginning to appreciate the fear I would have to overcome while chasing my dreams, but I was up for the challenge. "Not a chance, Mom," I replied to her comment. I had big dreams to live.

I did a couple hours of work before my stomach starting grumbling. I got up from the dining room table and walked to the fridge. Opening the door, I saw it was in its usual state of empty. While I had succeeded with some of the intentions I had set for my time in Victoria, maintaining a healthy diet had remained elusive. In the past, Rebecca and I had shared the cooking and shopping, so it wasn't like I didn't know what to do. But now that I was on my own, I had lost the motivation to spend the time shopping and cooking for one. It didn't seem like time well spent; I had so many other things I wanted to put that time towards. I recognized that was a mindset that still needed to be shifted.

The other challenge I was facing was the noise from the midday traffic outside my room. Over the month, the accumulating decibels from both the traffic outside, and the bar below, seemed to be compounding in my head. My stubborn desire for the corner suite had eclipsed all practicality. My ears were beginning to pay the price. In previous weeks, I could feel the stress building in my soul. The noise from the excavator on-site, when it was working, didn't help either. I still had so many thoughts I wanted to get clear in my mind. I had to find silence and I still had to eat. I decided to head out for lunch.

For lunch, I got a vegetarian dish from a nearby spot in Market Square. After lunch, I took a drive through town towards the ocean with hopes of finding silence. I parked along Dallas Road and made my way down the staircase to the cobble beach. It was midday during the week, so I was sure I would find serenity. I was wrong. The beach had several clusters of university students who must have just finished exams. They were keen on celebrating. I walked down the beach weaving between groups dancing to their portable stereos. I managed to find a space far enough away from the revelers. It wasn't perfect, but it would have to do. I took a seat against a large piece of driftwood.

In the bag that I was carrying I had brought my journal and *Evolve Your Brain*, by Dr. Joe. I reached into the bag and pulled out Dr. Joe to start. I read with fascination about neuroplasticity: how humans can repattern our brains to make a new sequence of circuitry. It sounded like walking a new path through a forest. At first the ground would be covered with leaves and the path would be unclear. But as one continued to walk the same path, a new route—or a new circuit—would form. In our brains this happened when we repeatedly thought in a different way. By thinking differently, we formed new neural connections. I recognized this applied in the same way to fear. When we kept repeating something that was at first intimidating, eventually, the fear would pass.

I took a break from reading to stare out at the ocean. Across the water I could see the snowy peaks of the Olympic Peninsula in Washington State. The sea rolled with a steady swell. Small waves were breaking across the rocky beach. Kelps beds were visible just offshore. The water was cold, and the abundance of ocean life gave off a pithy aroma. My time in Victoria was coming to an end. I had plans for the first part of my upcoming adventure, but nothing much beyond that. I had told my boss I would be back to work in Vancouver by July at the latest. My sentiments were honest, but I knew I had to find a way out of my current job. My best hope was through coaching.

As I looked out at the ocean, I reflected on how much had changed since the separation. In the beginning, my thirst for knowledge was driven by the need to understand what had happened to our marriage. The pain I experienced after the breakup motivated me to do everything possible to learn with hopes of never feeling that heartache again. I had learned about myself and the psychology that made humans happy. That was all I had wanted: to be happy again. I had diligently focused on learning and understanding. I attacked my new mission with more dedication than any prior work or school project. I had exercised the full extent of discipline I had built up over a lifetime of endurance sports: early morning swim practices during my pre-teen years, gruelling rowing workouts as a teenager, Ironman training in my early thirties, all of those experiences were training for this ultimate challenge. Everything in my life had led me to this point.

Two groups of students began to merge only feet away from where I was pondering life. With each alcoholic drink they consumed the volume on their stereos increased. My moment of Zen was over. I packed up my things and made my way back to the truck. It was still early in the day and I didn't want to go back to the loud hotel suite. I remembered there was a secluded beach out by the airport; without doubt, I could find quiet there.

Half an hour later I arrived at the next beach. I grabbed my bag and made my way out to the sand. I found a seat that had a great view of an island just offshore. The gulls were circling overhead, and the air was just warm enough to take off my shirt. The beach was long and largely deserted, except for a family that was playing a distance away. I was a little tired after the drive, so I closed my eyes and slouched down on the towel I had laid out. A midday oceanside nap in the sun; I was about to experience bliss. A lawnmower roared to life as I was about to touch sleep. It was only a few metres behind me, on the field between the beach and the parking lot. I turned in disbelief to see a park maintenance worker happily cutting a grid through the overgrown grass. "You've got to be kidding me," I grumbled to myself. I packed up and walked back to the truck.

The Universe was trying to teach me something on one of my final days in Victoria. I was ready to accept the lesson, but I was running out of beaches. I had one beach left near my old university. I got back in the truck and started the drive back towards town.

I arrived a half-hour later. After parking, I made the short walk through the parking lot towards the beach. I was grateful there were no throngs of students or roaring lawnmowers. I found my third patch of beach for the day and unloaded my books. Looking out across Cadboro Bay I saw a small fleet of sailboats from the nearby yacht club. It was at that same yacht club, some twenty years earlier, where I had my first experience in Victoria. At the time, I was visiting from Ontario for a sailing training camp.

My mind drifted back to the girl I was dating at that time. A fellow team member, we had met the summer before at a regatta. Just like my marriage, the relationship had ended with me in a pile of hurt. I had been crushed, but I hadn't learned anything from that experience. Sitting on the beach I wondered, what exactly was the lesson I should have learned? Why was I repeatedly attracting the wrong type of partner?

Recently I had learned, through the Law of Attraction, that we attract what we are. Perhaps I had been attracting the wrong type of partner because I had been projecting an inauthentic version of myself. In the past, maybe I wasn't being true to myself, projecting a caged, closed, egotistical existence. When deep down I wanted to fully express myself, chase big dreams, and help others. All those years, I must have been attracting partners who were compatible with an inauthentic version of myself. No wonder none of the relationships had lasted... I wasn't being real. A lump formed in my throat with the clarity of the realization. It took courage to take complete ownership for how my life had unfolded—something I didn't have some twenty years earlier when fear had stopped me from discovering my truths. I hoped I had finally learned my lesson by facing those same fears.

———————

My last day in Victoria came midway through the following week. I spent the final morning packing my things in the suite. Over the previous days, work on-site had got back on track after the excavator was repaired. It was bittersweet to hand off my duties to a co-worker, since I would not be able to see the final days of our hole being filled. Then again, the hole was underwater—there wasn't much to see.

My final task before checking out of the hotel was a call with Brittany. Her voice still wasn't healed, so she continued to communicate by text while I talked. On the call she challenged me to make sure my upcoming trip was purposeful. "You won't accomplish your goals lying around the beach all day," she texted.

"Yes, coach," I said.

"I want you to spend your time purposefully; listen to podcasts while you travel, practice telling your story as you walk the beaches, visualize yourself speaking in front of massive audiences. One of your main goals of this trip is to find your voice. You want to come back from this trip ready to share your story, in a big way."

"Yes, I agree. And the book, I've got to start working on the book. I've been writing lines in my head when I run, now it's time to get it down on paper."

"Yes, you must keep this momentum going, you must stay focused. You will only go as far as your mind will take you, Michael."

Halfway through the call we switched to talk about starting my coaching business. Brittany wanted me to focus on creating impactful social media content that would attract future clients. She reiterated how important it was to be vulnerable and share how I had overcome my challenges.

"Do not worry about offending people. Speak and post as if you are talking to one person, your ideal client. Speak the truth and have no sensors. People will not understand you; they won't accept you; they won't agree with you; do not let it affect you. You can accept and love them for who they are, but you must remain in control, and you must have rock solid confidence."

"It all comes back to confidence, eh?"

"Yes, Michael, confidence is everything. Especially when facing your fears and going in new directions."

After the call I sat in silence on the living room couch. Like the loft I had stayed in for February and March, the suite had been an exquisite space for my continued evolution. Despite the noise from the bar below and the traffic outside, the original art and exposed wood beams had created an energy that was perfect for my daily contemplation.

I had accomplished my main mission during my three months in Victoria by getting clearer on who I was. By working through my own healing process, I had discovered the ability to help others through their challenges. I had continued to strengthen my mental discipline, focusing on removing bad habits, like drinking. I had worked hard on connecting with others by listening and feeling what they were experiencing. I had gotten two more tattoos to symbolize that important time in my life. I had, for the most part, kept up with my New Year's resolution of being present. I was getting further clarity on a new life I wanted to create that included coaching, speaking, and writing. I was beginning to learn that everything I wanted to achieve, lay on the other side of facing my fears.

I had spent the previous week making the final arrangements before my trip south. All the loose ends with work had been tied up and I was free to close my mind on my time in Victoria. At the same time, I was ready to fully immerse myself in whatever awaited me in Central America.

It took several trips to transport my mountain of gear from the suite to the truck. I was booked on an early afternoon ferry to Vancouver. I would stay two days in Vancouver before catching a flight to Nicaragua. As I carried out the last of my bags, I saw two older homeless men in wheelchairs near the truck. The truck was already full of most of my stuff. My instinctive reaction was one of suspicion. As I got closer, I realized the two men were harmless.

I approached the truck and one of them wheeled his chair behind a nearby dumpster. I watched as the remaining fellow started to follow his friend. He saw that I was trying to piece together what they were up to. "I got to go help him pee, he needs my help," he said.

"You're a good friend," I replied.

"It's what I do. I help him."

"He is lucky to have you. You know that, right?"

"It's nothing. We are supposed to help each other. That's what we are here for, ya know?"

"Yes, I am slowly learning that."

"Also," he paused and looked into the sky before continuing his thought, "I'd like to think that the people looking back from the space station see a planet where every man helps each other."

"Amen, brother. I like the sound of that."

He started to wheel away before stopping and turning to me. He looked me in the eye and said, "We can't change the world, ya know, but at least I can help my buddy."

He disappeared behind the dumpster to help his friend. I loaded the last of my gear into the truck. As I drove out of the parking lot and made my way out of town, I realized that what he had said was not entirely true. By being there for his buddy each day, he wasn't just helping him, the impact that he was making through his service was in fact changing his buddy's world. It was a surprisingly beautiful final moment to end my time in Victoria. A feeling of love washed over me as I drove out of town. Carrying that love, I was ready to face the next part of my journey, and all the fears that came with it.

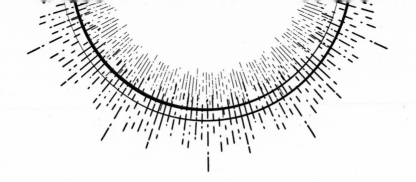

CHAPTER 13

LOVE

*The world is my country, all mankind are my brethren,
and to do good is my religion.*

THOMAS PAINE

The surf camp was located in the northwestern corner of Nicaragua. After months of living in solitude back home, I struggled during the first few days. Although the compound was spread over multiple buildings, I found it challenging to be spending so much time amongst the twenty other guests. I still felt somewhat fragile; like I was guarding the energy and confidence I had worked so hard to rebuild. At the same time, I was in a foreign land where no one knew me, so I was able to step further into the new life I was creating. When I introduced myself to the others at the camp, I would say that I was a coach and a writer. Even though I had just started, it felt good to speak my new life into existence.

The days passed with a glorious mix of meditation, surfing, and yoga. It was an adjustment from the busy life I had back in Canada. In between surf sessions and yoga classes we had plenty of free time. Most of the others—the majority of whom were also in their thirties, including a high percentage of female doctors—hung out by the pool. The first few days I joined them to learn more about their lives. There were only a few other guys in the group. At times, as we rotated around getting to know the women, it seemed as though we were on own version of *The Bachelor* TV show. Except hooking up with someone for a few days wasn't my focus. I was there to catch waves, but I was also on a mission to start my book.

As the week went on, I snuck away on the breaks to write. Over the previous days of travel, I had read Stephen King's *On Writing*[11] and *Ernest Hemingway On Writing*[12] by Larry W. Phillips (Editor). I had no idea where to start, and figured those books were as good a place as any. After I finished the books, I began reviewing my journal entries, which started six months earlier in November. I felt heavy and sad re-entering those dark days. More than once tears formed in my eyes, as I was transported back into my own troubled mind.

It only took a day or two to find my rhythm. I was focused on King's advice to write one thousand words each day. I made notes as I read through my journal entries. I used my day planner to cross reference past dates. I even used my social media history to remember what I had been thinking at the time. I wrote by hand for two to three hours every day into the Moleskine books I had brought on the trip. As I wrote, tropical birds serenaded me from the nearby trees. By slowly

---

11   King, Stephen. *On Writing: A Memoir of the Craft*. Scribner, 2010.

12   Phillips, Larry W. (editor). *Ernest Hemingway on Writing*. Scribner, 1999.

working through each page in my journals, I got closer to better understanding all that I had been through. With each heartbreaking journal page I turned, I got closer to closure on that part of my life.

On our surf outings, we divided into smaller groups. Towards the end of the week, our advanced crew of six loaded into a boat to access a remote left-hand point break. We were all super stoked to ride uncrowded waves. When we arrived at the break, the tide was still too low to form surfable waves. The shallow depths were causing the waves to build to double overhead, before closing out in a thunderous roar. They weren't the best conditions, but we knew the tide was coming up and the waves would soon improve.

Eventually, we got tired of waiting. We all jumped out of the boat and paddled slowly towards the break. Conditions were still ugly, so we stayed on the outside of the breaking waves. After half an hour or so I grew impatient and paddled closer to shore to catch a wave. Once I was on the inside, I saw a set of large waves approaching. I was in too deep. No matter how hard I paddled I could not get back to safety on the outside. I was going to pay the price for my impatience. I managed to paddle over the top of the first two waves in the set, but I couldn't escape the third. The wave picked me up before tossing me deep into its churning dark froth. I was only pulled under for a few seconds, but it felt like an eternity. During those moments I couldn't tell which way was up, or if I was going to get crushed into the rocks below.

The wave slowly started to release its grip on me. Still submerged, I instinctively pulled my right leg to engage the leash that was attached to my board. Usually when I did that motion, the leash would tighten, and the board would float me to the surface. But on that occasion, there was nothing to pull against. The leash was still attached to my leg, but there didn't seem to be anything attached on the other end. I instantly panicked. My one piece of floatation, the surfboard, seemed to no longer be connected to me. My soul and I had become untethered.

I managed to struggle to the surface for a half-breath before the next wall of water pulled me under. I was used to getting pulled under by waves, but never without the security of my board. The unfamiliar feeling was terrifying, especially considering the others were still a distance away, unaware that I was in danger. Again, I scrambled to the surface to grab a bigger breath before the ensuing wave hit. The next time I came to the surface, I again pulled on my leash and was relieved to see that it was still attached to a small piece of my board. The rest of the board had snapped off from the power of the wave. I carefully positioned the broken board with the splintered fiberglass edges underneath my chest. My heart was still pounding as I started to swim my way back towards the safety of the boat.

My adrenaline was still pumping as I pulled myself out of the water and into the boat. I sat taking deep breaths with my head resting in my hands. I had survived. My board, on the other hand, was a write-off; the other half now washed up on shore. The board could be easily replaced, but my nerves were shattered. My mind started to drift towards what would have happened if I hadn't gotten those first few breaths. We were miles from any medical services, in a remote corner of a Third World country. I shuddered at the thought: what would it have meant to lose it all? I had only recently started to turn my life around. I was getting clearer on the new life I wanted to create. I had been building excitement around chasing my dreams. In an instant, I had almost lost it all.

With the others still in the water, I continued to sit in gratitude in the safety of the boat. I had never loved any boat more in my life. My impatience had taught me a hard lesson. The same impatience that had created unrealistic expectations during my conference talk back in Seattle. At the time, I thought I was skilled enough to give an outstanding talk. The muted reaction from the audience had suggested otherwise. I knew I wanted to be a great speaker, but I would have to be patient as I developed the skills to do so. An even bigger gap existed between my actual surfing skills and what I thought I was capable of in my mind.

Since I had gotten out of the water, the tide had risen and the others were starting to catch some good waves. The point break which we had come for started to produce gorgeous peeling waves—the likes of which I had never seen back in Canada.

Our guide paddled over to the boat to check on me and my crushed confidence.

"You alright, bru?" he asked.

"Well, I am now," I said.

"It's looking pretty good out there, are you ready to dive back in?"

"Well, I've got a bit of an equipment issue," I said, referring to my broken board.

"Ah, no worries, you're welcome to use mine."

"I don't know, I'm not sure I'm ready to get back in there."

"Dude, when are you going to get this opportunity again? You are in paradise, the waves are perfect, you got this, brother."

He was right. I was probably never going to surf this break again in my life. My confidence had been crushed, as it had been months earlier with the separation. But similar to how I had rebuilt my confidence after the breakup, I was going to have to dive back into the water and face my fears. "Alright man, I'm ready," I said, as I took his board and jumped into the water.

I paddled back out to join the others. They were catching wave after wave and celebrating with arms overhead at the end of each ride. I slowly inched myself towards the takeoff point. I saw a wave approach and I paddled with all my might. The wave lifted me from behind and I pushed the board down the face of the wave as I rose to my feet. The wave was bigger than I was used to, but it was too late to jump off. I started to scream down the glassy surface as the height of the wave built behind me. The guide's board was smaller and faster than any board I had ever ridden. I held my balance and rode the wave all the way to shore. It was the best wave of my life.

I grinned ear to ear as I paddled back out to catch another wave. Just like I had survived hitting rock bottom after the separation, I had endured the ferocity of the ocean. And just as courage had kept me moving forward during my dark days, it had now rewarded me with the ride of my life.

―――――――――

The week at the surf camp was followed by a move south to stay with my sister and her family. Jenn sensed that I was on a mission, so she set me up in the secluded casita, a small guest house, away from the main buildings. The casita was a perfect sanctuary. The natural woods and wraparound screens connected me deeply with the nearby jungle.

Most mornings I woke up shortly after five as nature came to life. Birds and howler monkeys called between their perches in the nearby trees. A light wind rolled through the nearby treetops carrying a tropical mist through the screens of the casita. At night, the evening rains lulled me to sleep tapping the roof overhead. I continued my routine of writing two to three hours each day. In between writing sessions, I meditated, turning my mind towards refining the future life I wanted to live.

While we were enjoying the peace of the jungle, the rest of the country was unraveling in civil unrest. The Nicaraguan government had recently made changes to the country's federal pension plan. Led by a passionate group of students, demonstrations against the government had been escalating over the previous weeks. The protests had been met with violence by the government-backed paramilitaries who were fighting the young protestors. We had all been aware of the situation before flying down but were hoping that things wouldn't escalate. Where we were in the country was safe for the time being, but we remained on high alert.

Jenn spoke daily with her local contacts to better understand the evolving situation. Dinner-time conversations were dominated by *what-ifs* and scheming backup plans of escaping to neighbouring Costa Rica. With the trajectory of the civil unrest unknown, we prepared for the worst by stockpiling extra cash, food, and water. The fear was that banks could close, supplies would run out, or the situation could escalate quickly, forcing us to make a run for the border. The tension was compounded by rolling power failures. Added to the challenges were our constant high alert for scorpions, spiders, and snakes. Our degree of Zen was somewhat tempered.

Even with the uncertainty of the civil unrest and the poisonous critters, the casita became the perfect space to do my work. In addition to the writing, I was doing a couple hours a day maintaining engineering projects back home. I also built my coaching website and a landing page for the just-started book. I had no concept of how long it would take to write a book, but I knew I worked best under a deadline. Across the top of the landing page I wrote: "Coming This Fall". It was naively optimistic, being only a few months away, but I needed a target to shoot for.

Unfortunately for my sister, as news of the civil unrest grew, the requests for rentals on her property shrank. The setback for my sister was a blessing for me: if the country stayed safe enough, I could stay in the casita through the end of June, after they left at the beginning of the month. At the pace I was writing, I figured I could get a draft done by then.

As the days passed, we witnessed the winter dry season turn to spring green. Nightly rains transformed the parched landscape into a lush green jungle. Along with an invasion of insects, the rains awakened vibrant yellow blossoms in the jungle trees. The flowers showed their best colours in the early morning. The rising sun would reflect off the lingering moisture from the previous night's rain. Along with the pleasant and peaceful rains, came occasional powerful thunderstorms. One night, during my second week in the casita, an especially strong storm made me feel as though I was in a ship getting tossed on the high seas.

Heavy wind and rain mixed with a relentless torrent of lightning and thunder. I huddled alone in my bed as flashes of light pulsed through the screen walls. The wind blew a fine mist through the screens, slowly drenching me in bed. I was too thrilled by the excitement of the storm to think what else might be getting soaked in the casita.

The next morning, I got out of bed and walked across the damp floor towards the dining area. I gasped when saw that my stack of journals on the dining table had also got soaked. Included within the journals were three weeks' worth of manuscript writing that I had already completed. I was ready to accept that all my work had been lost. I had nobody to blame but myself. I would even consider it a sign from the Universe if everything had been lost—maybe I was supposed to start again, maybe it wasn't good enough, maybe the story just wasn't meant to be told. Thankfully, that wasn't the case.

The night before I had placed the Moleskine journal, on which I had started the manuscript, inside a larger hardcover journal. The hardcover journal was the same notebook I had first recorded those first painful days back in November. At that time, I had used whiteout to scrawl across the front of the book the capital letters: HELL. It was the only word I could use to describe those days. Later, as my darkness started to lift, I added an O to the letters, as if to say *hello* to the new world I was stepping into. The same journal that had helped me sort through those dark days, had somehow fully preserved the first chapters of the manuscript.

On nights when storms weren't raging, I retreated to the casita after dinner to enjoy the solitude. I was serenaded by distant waves crashing against the shore, and faint reggae music from houses across the valley. The peaceful melody blended with the natural chorus from the jungle. It was during this time that I dove deeply into Dr. Joe's *Becoming Supernatural*. The more I read, the more I found explanations about what had been changing in my mind.

Dr. Joe explained that the degree of your transformation must be greater than your sadness. For me, back in those early days, my desire to return to happiness was greater than the sadness I experienced after the breakup. I knew I didn't want to stay in the pain. I believed I could find a way to move forward. It hadn't been easy, and my heart still ached at times, but I wasn't going to let myself rot in anguish.

I learned more about manifesting dreams from Dr. Joe. Ever since the fleeting moment at the surfside café, I had been digging deeper into manifesting. Night after night in the casita I studied manifestation meditations. In one of his exercises, Dr. Joe suggested to start the meditation visualizing a letter of the alphabet that was meaningful. With this letter in your mind's eye, you added a series of energetic rings pulsing around it. The next step was to think about your intentions for your dream life, or what you wanted to manifest. The last step was to feel the elevated emotions that would be present when your dreams manifested.

I chose the letter T to place at the centre of my energized rings. My intentions for my dream life had become clearer during my travels: I saw myself as a bestselling author, traveling the world speaking on a book tour, in the company of friends, family and my soulmate. To that vision I added the emotions of joy, freedom, love, gratitude, and bliss. I spent hours in that state nestled in the casita.

To get my meditations started, I would do a head-to-toe body scan over a series of several breaths. Sitting with eyes closed, I'd start with my awareness at the top of my head and the space surrounding it. With each deep breath I would scan down—on the exhale—over one portion of my body. I started at the top of my head then moved to my right shoulder, right arm, then right hand. Over the next three breaths, I would move to my left shoulder, left arm, then left hand. Next, I would scan through my chest and stomach, before reaching my pelvis. From there I would move down to my right leg, right calf, then to my right foot. I would finish the scan over a series of three breaths moving down my left leg, left calf, to my left foot. Once the scan was complete, I would do a full scan from my head to my toes over the course of one exhale. I repeated the full body scan three times. The scans started to become so powerful that I could energize my body simply through my breath and awareness.

Next, I would move through a series of energetic inhales to illuminate the seven energy centres, or chakras, along my spine. I started with my awareness at the base of my pelvis, then moved to my sacrum, solar plexus, heart, throat, third eye, before ending at the crown of my head. On the inhale, I would squeeze the breath up through my spinal cord while visualizing a ball of light illuminating each chakra. I would do one powerful inhale for each energy centre. On the exhales, I would focus my attention on the space between the back of my head and my throat, where the pineal gland was located. Dr. Joe had stated that pineal gland was our antenna to the Universe. To finish, I would take three powerful inhales, making sure all seven chakras were fully lit as I squeezed the breath out through the top of my head.

By this point in the meditation my whole body was vibrating. I'd pull into my mind's eye my letter T and think about my intentions of becoming a bestselling author, traveling the world with friends, family, and my soulmate. I'd match these intentions by feeling the most amazing sensations of joy, freedom, love, and gratitude. Bliss would wash over my vibrating body. The whole meditation took about twenty minutes. It was a powerful exercise that I repeated daily.

Early into the practice, a very clear scene repeatedly came into my mind. As I sat flooded with energized bliss, I would see in my mind's eye a white rooftop deck overlooking a turquoise harbour. It seemed like a Mediterranean scene with boats bobbing in the waters below. The light was low, as it was early evening, the air warm with a light breeze. My friends, family and soulmate joined me around a long outdoor table for dinner in the fading daylight. The scene was filled with food, music, laughter, and smiles. It was a celebration of the book tour and the positive impact that was being made.

I returned to this scene often during my meditations. On some occasions I would have incredible experiences where my meditating self would talk with my future self. For my meditating self, it was as though I was talking to the big brother I never had. I looked up to my future self. He was strong, calm, poised, dignified, just like mountains I had visualized in previous meditations. He had everything he desired, everything we desired: success, impact, connection, and love. Future me would always tell meditating me to trust our journey, be patient, that we were on the right path. I knew that one day I would be in his shoes.

During other meditations I would experience my future self, having a conversation with my future partner. I could never make out her face, but I could always feel the love and trust between us. We were consciously creating the life of our dreams. Her beauty radiated from every pore of her being. Those meditations would end as we shared a passionate kiss. I always felt so much love.

———————

Jenn and her family left as planned during the first week of June. My plan was to stay until the end of the month so I could finish the manuscript. I was making progress each day, working through my volumes of journals. It was slow going, but I savoured those hours lost in thought each day. Through the process, I was gaining a better understanding of how my story had unfolded over the previous months. At the same time as I wrote about my transformation, the jungle was undergoing a change of its own. With each passing day it came more to life. Combined with the energy of the distant waves crashing ashore, a seemingly perfect vortex of peaceful energy was directed right into the casita. I was living a deep-seated dream of writing my book in a secluded, tropical nirvana.

My first night alone was timed with the arrival of the loudest creatures in the jungle: the frogs. Their chorus reached an almost deafening volume as they searched for their next mate. It was too loud to sleep, so for the first time in months I sat down to watch TV.

I set the volume on high to drown out the frogs and loaded Tony Robbins' Netflix special, *I Am Not Your Guru*. The show followed the greatest coach in the business through one of his multiday events. Tony described how coaching was designed for people who were hungry for more out of their lives. He explained that the best way to unleash our full potential was to break the pattern of who we are. I had heard others describe how we were born connected to our true selves. But we often got lost along the way with responsibilities, social influence, or adulting. That made sense and I wondered if that had happened to me. At my core I wondered if I really was that blonde kid that used to run wild through the streets. Had the connection to the real me been masked by careers, mortgages, and a marriage? Had I lost myself by taking life too seriously?

As I considered the possibility, Tony said something that changed my life when he said: "Life is happening for us, not to us." I paused the show to think on his statement. It was a paradigm shift. Instead of being a victim to all of life's challenges, Tony was suggesting that the same challenges were a gift to serve our personal evolution. It had taken me months to come to the realization that the separation had been a catalyst to awaken parts of me that had been dormant. Tony's words put my life in a new perspective: all of my challenges: my parent's divorce, the struggles in my engineering career, even the physical pain of doing an Ironman, all of it had happened for me, to help me grow and reach my full potential.

With each passing day the civil unrest continued to escalate in other parts of the country. The violence had started to move closer to me, but I remained safe for the time being. Some of the demonstrations were preventing supplies from getting through. So, on the first Tuesday in June, I caught a bus into town to stock up on food.

I hadn't been to town in over a week, and I was surprised to see that it was largely empty of tourists. While I moved throughout the town, I overheard rumblings from the locals about the fragile state of the country. The weight of my duffle bag grew with each stop. I bumped into a local I had befriended, as my bag reached an unbearable weight. She was on her own resupply mission and I was grateful when she offered me a ride home in her truck.

On our way out of town we stopped at a shop so she could get her usual supply of drinking water. I waited in the truck while she went inside. She came out less than a minute later, without any water. As she climbed back into the truck, she told me that the supply trucks couldn't pass the barricades in other parts of the country. The situation was really starting to escalate. We drove on to a second shop to see if they had any water. They did not. On our third try, we found water at a small shop just outside of town. "There's bad energy in the air today," she said, as we loaded the water into her truck, "Really bad. There are faces in town that I do not recognize. Those guys we passed a little way back, I didn't recognize them."

The violence that had shaken other parts of the country was moving closer. I could tell from the tone in her voice that something had shifted. She was a strong woman, a local surf star and masseuse. To hear the fear in her voice made me wonder what I was still doing in the country.

I awoke the next morning to a moody overcast sky. The weight of the tropical clouds added to the bad energy in the air. The power had been out all night, which meant that my means of communicating with the outside world had been cut. I had barely slept. I was grateful to see the power back on in the morning. I turned on my phone to check for any updates.

My sister had forwarded me a message from her local contact. It read: "Your brother should leave. Immediately." The message continued and warned of rumours that the paramilitaries were kidnapping the student protestors, taking hostages, and burning buildings. If the violence continued to escalate, banks would be closing and food, water, and gas shortages could be expected. It was time to go.

Over the course of the day, I packed my things and made a plan to go to neighbouring Costa Rica. By the next morning I was safely on a bus headed for the border. I was grateful to have the option to flee; it was a privilege that others didn't have. Before I left, I did my best to communicate to the groundskeeper that he could have all the food I had just bought. Despite the language barrier, we had bonded during my stay. He understood why I had to go, but the mood was sombre the morning I left. I was one of the last guests to leave the houses under his care. My departure and the growing uncertainty in the country meant that his job was in jeopardy. Even if he and his family had had passports, which they didn't, they didn't have the means to escape the country if the situation deteriorated further. It was with a heavy heart that I left the country that had been so good to me.

At the same time, it was a real blessing to have Costa Rica one country to the south. I could even feel the change in the energy once I crossed the border. For days, the tension in Nicaragua had been building; the air had become charged with negative energy. Upon arriving in Costa Rica, I felt safer and the air felt calm and peaceful.

On the recommendation of great waves, my first stop was Playa Grande. I had been spoiled with my own casita at Jenn's, so the rustic surf hostel took a little getting used to. The lack of privacy meant I had to be creative to stick with my productive routine. While the other guests fueled their days with booze and parties, I took to the beach to continue my writing. There was no shade on the beach, so most days I would gather large palm leaves and create a shelter from the sun. It was awkward to write lying in the sand, but it was the best I could do.

It was during the week at Playa Grande that Brittany gave me access to her collection of eBooks. We had reduced the frequency of our calls because of my travels, but we were still in touch by text. She wanted me to use my free time to accelerate my intake of knowledge. When I logged into her collection, I was blown away to find hundreds of books on self-help, coaching, relationships, public speaking, psychology, spirituality, health, and wealth. The first book I downloaded was Robert Greene's, *Mastery*[13]. The book examined the lives of historical figures and what led to their success. It was the perfect company during my long beach walks.

I stayed ten days in Playa Grande before moving south to Playa Negra. Since the start of my trip back in May, I had been considering doing a yoga teacher training while I was in Central America. I was interested in learning more about how the practice of yoga affects both our bodies and our minds. I had decided not to sign up for the training, since my focus was on writing. But the thought had been percolating in the back of my mind. So, I wasn't too surprised when I arrived at my next accommodation and learned that a yoga teacher training was already in progress. I was beginning to master manifestation.

---

13 Greene, Robert. *Mastery*. Penguin Books, 2013.

The owners of the Peace Retreat and the facilitators of the training were kind enough to invite me to join the others for daily meditations and yoga sessions. I found myself choosing to spend my days lingering around the peaceful property, instead of walking to the nearby ocean. I used the opportunity to fully connect with my meditations and to try and understand why the Universe had brought me to such a serene environment.

Considering where my life had been only half a year earlier, I could never have imagined ending up at such a beautiful place. Every cell in my body was experiencing a level of peace like never before. The feeling was a great contrast to the previous pain, grief, and sorrow I had felt. But perhaps one extreme couldn't have existed without the other.

I had been through so much, yet I had survived. I had worked so hard to try to understand what had gone wrong. I had put my everything into moving forward one day at a time. I had overcome hurdle after hurdle with the help of so many. There were still countless unknowns about where I was headed and I was still spending time with the darkness, where I had further lessons to learn. But for the most part, I had found peace: peace with what had happened and peace within myself.

A light rain started to fall late one afternoon as I made my way to the outdoor yoga studio. I entered the studio and set up a mat in the centre of the space. I took a seat on a bolster while being serenaded by a harmony of birds, monkeys, and a distant rumbling of thunder. I closed my eyes and began to scan my body. I placed my awareness at the top of my head and the space around it. I slowly moved down my body over a series of deep breaths. With the scan complete, I moved on to igniting my energy centres over a series of powerful inhales while squeezing the air from my pelvis through the crown of my head. On each inhale I visualized igniting a ball of light around each of my chakras. It didn't take long for me to tap into what the Universe wanted me to feel.

My mind drifted to my sister Jenn. The situation in Nicaragua was affecting the people she loved so deeply. She had fallen in love with the country and its beautiful people. She had also given me so much love with her support over the previous months. I sent all my love to her as I repeated the words in my mind: *I love you. I love you. I love you.*

Next, I thought of Dad. I pictured him sitting with his dogs in his living room back in Kingston. I started to sob as I thought about him. I desperately hoped he knew how much my sisters and I appreciated everything he did for us. I knew my separation had been hard on him. I knew it hurt him to see me suffer. I wanted him to know how much he meant to me and that everything was going to work out. I held a vision of him in my mind as I repeated the words: *I love you. I love you. I love you.*

I thought of Mom, my Ironmom. She was a warrior who had instilled within me a strength and determination that I was only beginning to understand. She had waited up for me on Christmas Day after all my travel delays and welcomed me home when I needed her the most. She just wanted her kids to be happy; we only wanted the same for her. I thought of Mom and whispered: *I love you. I love you. I love you.*

Then I thought of my younger sister, Jane. I knew it had been hard for her seeing my pain while at the same time living her dream of becoming a mom. Neither of us thought she would have kids before I did. What she didn't know was how much joy I felt seeing the light her boy had brought to her eyes. A light that she had always been searching for. The tears continued as I thought of her: *I love you. I love you. I love you.*

Finally, I thought of myself. I thought of the broken soul that had spent night after night sobbing on the living room floor. I thought about all the tear-filled dinners with friends and family. I thought about how scared I had been to start living alone. I thought about the courage it had taken to repeatedly ask for help. I thought about how good it had felt to start stepping back into the light with the moments of satori. I thought about how good it was going to feel as that light continued to brighten towards a life of bliss, ananda. A smile slowly inched across my face as I softly mouthed the words: *I love you. I love you. I love you.*

The tears came to a stop as I slowly opened my eyes. The sky had grown dark during my meditation. I sat motionless in the centre of the studio. I was fully connected with the nature that surrounded me. Soft flashes of lightning danced across the sky. I knew it was the Universe winking at me. I knew it was a sign that I was on the right path. I knew why my journey had brought me here: it was to feel love.

Love from friends and family had got me through my pain.

Love was what I felt when connected to nature.

Love was what I felt when I sat in silence.

Love was what the Universe was made of.

It is that same love, that will awaken the world to happiness.

My awakening had shone a light on the self-serving parts of my personality that I didn't want to carry forward. By embracing the journey to go within, I was able to find peace in the present moment. Once I got clear on the new me, I shed everything that prevented him from fully emerging. I continued to build my awareness muscle to navigate the higher highs and the lower lows of the emotional extremes. I experienced a transformational shift in perspective when I stopped acting like a victim and switched my mindset to see how everything in my life had happened for a reason.

Subconsciously, I had asked for this wakeup call; when it came, I had to generate enough courage to answer it. Through building my mental discipline I started to focus my mind on consciously creating my future and stepping into the light. I learned to be alone but not lonely, but also realized that meaningful connections made my heart sing.

I transcended my pain to find my purpose: to use my words and my voice to inspire others. I had learned so much from my transformation; it was my calling, my dharma, to lead others through transformations of their own. The stillness of meditation allowed me to connect with my soul's deepest desires and the life of my dreams. I could see the pathway to the stages I had always wanted. As my dreams grew, so did the fear that tried to hold me back.

My deep connection with nature helped me feel the highest forms of love vibrating from the Universe. I was already having success manifesting my dream life—it was obvious what to do next: focus on love and start to dream bigger.

BOOKS READ ON THIS JOURNEY

Singer, Michael A. *The Untethered Soul: The Journey Beyond Yourself.*
New Harbinger Publications, 2007.

Tolle, Eckhart. *A New Earth: Awakening to Your Life's Purpose.*
Penguin Life, 2008.

Goleman, Daniel, & Davidson, Richard J. *Altered Traits: Science
Reveals How Meditation Changes Your Mind, Brain, and Body.* Avery,
2017.

Kaur, Rupi. *Milk & Honey.* Andrews McMeel Publishing, 2015.

Kaur, Rupi. *The Sun and Her Flowers.* Simon & Schuster, 2017.

Kiedis, Anthony. *Scar Tissue.* Hachette Books, 2005.

Junger, Sebastian. *Tribe: On Becoming and Belonging.* Twelve, 2016.

Siegel, Daniel J. *The Developing Mind: How Relationships and the
Brain Interact to Shape Who We Are.* The Guilford Press, 2001.

Dispenza, Joe. *Evolve Your Brain: The Science of Changing Your Mind.*
Health Communications Inc, 2008.

Dispenza, Joe. *Becoming Supernatural: How Common People are Doing the Uncommon.* Hay House Inc, 2017.

King, Stephen. *On Writing: A Memoir of the Craft.* Scribner, 2010.

Phillips, Larry W. (editor). *Ernest Hemingway on Writing.* Scribner, 1999.

Greene, Robert. *Mastery.* Penguin Books, 2013.

EXPERTS REFERENCED IN THIS BOOK

Gord Downie

Dalai Lama

Reinhold Niebuhr

Buddha

C. Assaad

davidji

Wim Hof

Esther Perel

Tony Robbins

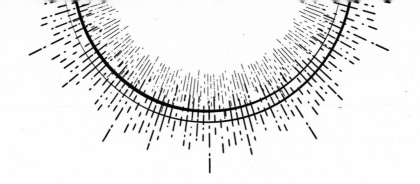

ACKNOWLEDGMENTS

This has been a humbling yet highly rewarding experience.

Firstly, I wish to thank my team of editors. Each one of these brave souls helped this piece of writing grow from a pile of well-traveled journals, into the work you are holding in your hands. They also helped guide a left-brained thinker into the world of writing.

The team of Stacey Covell & Chantel Hamilton answered my call for help at exactly the right time. Your professional touch was firm enough to help me grow as a writer, but not too hard that I quit in despair. I wish to thank you both for your patience and also your enthusiasm for this project. I love you and I thank you.

During the early weeks of the pandemic, a dedicated crew showed up every night for two and a half weeks to listen to my live readings. I cannot express just how much this meant to me. Your commitment and your interest were unexpected but deeply appreciated. Knowing that you were showing up each night was exactly what I needed to advance the edits. I love you and I thank you: Max, Kristy, Charlotte, Monika, Nick, Lorinder & David.

My beta readers, where did you guys even come from? I was blown away by the contributions each of you made and how you improved the writing with your love. On top of that, you put up with my artificial deadlines, repeated poking, and multiple just-one-more-questions. I love you and I thank you: Dad, Adam, Kristina, Karen, Sinead.

I tasked Sylvia Taylor with a highly engineered set of instructions to perform the final edit. Thankfully, she wisely revised them and proceeded to give the writing the perfect final touch. I want to thank you for sharing my passion on this project and also your patience (is this a theme?) with me. I love you and I thank you.

I had no idea how Laura Wrubleski was going to transform my vision for the cover design out of my head and onto paper. Thankfully, it wasn't an exact replica, rather a combination of my vision and her brilliant expertise as a designer. Laura, I love the cover, as I know many others will. Like those mentioned above, thank you for silently nodding along to my list of errant requests, then ultimately providing exactly what I needed. I love you and I thank you.

Suzanne Doyle-Ingram has been with me from the beginning. Ever since that first day we met on Granville Island and I stood in front of the crowd and proclaimed, "I'm writing a New York Times Bestseller!" You have provided timely support at each stage of this journey, especially the final step where this book entered the world representing Prominence

Publishing. I love you and I thank you.

To all my brothers and sisters in the Evolutionary Business Council: I can't even imagine where I would be without your guidance, support and expertise. I am repeatedly in awe about how I fell into your world (that same day on Granville Island when I met Suzanne). You have helped me enter a world that I didn't know existed, and have done so with radiant open hearts. I love you all and I look forward to thanking each of you for your encouragement to "just keep going" with this project.

To Mom, Dad, Jenn & Jane. I don't think any of us appreciate how fortunate we are to have each other. To have a family that will always be there, unconditionally, is truly a blessing. Each one of you was with me every step of the way. You supported me in your own unique ways, always at the right time. I'm not sure how many books it's going to take to say all I want to say, but I'll always know you'll support my dreams. I really love you guys.

Lastly, I wish to acknowledge every soul I connected with along this journey. When I told you I was writing my story, your face would light up. The excitement that reflected back from your eyes was all the inspiration I needed to press on. I really am grateful for all the amazing connections that were made. I am beyond excited for the connections that are yet to come. I love each and every one of you and I thank you.

Sending an abundance of love, and then some more.

Please visit www.michaeltranmer.com/meditation to access your free guided meditation.

The *awaken to happiness* meditation is the same meditation that I used in the book (and most days since) during my travels through Central America. I wanted to create a version for you to also tap into the magic. The meditation is suitable for both advanced and beginner meditators.

In this three-part meditation you will be guided to:

- Use your breath and awareness to rinse any energy that no longer serves you.

- Energize your body by igniting each one of your chakras—the seven energy centers that run along your spine.

- Match your clear intentions with elevated emotions to manifest the life of your dreams.

By the end of the meditation you will be vibrating.

I know you'll love it,

Michael

ABOUT THE AUTHOR

Michael holds a Bachelor's degree in Mechanical Engineering, a Master's degree in Coastal Engineering, and is a Project Management Professional. As a Professional Engineer, Michael specializes in the complex field of Coastal Engineering, leading multidisciplinary teams on multimillion-dollar projects throughout coastal British Columbia. Michael's specialty is facilitating effective communication and coaching team members to transcend beyond their limitations to achieve personal and professional greatness.

His personal development training includes the Evolutionary Business Council's Certified Master Trainer Program, the Power of Success with Tony Robbins, and High-Performance Academy

& Experts Academy with Brendon Burchard. Michael is a TEDx speaking coach and a Certified Coach Practitioner with the Certified Coaches Federation.

Michael embodies and speaks on Transcendent Leadership, drawing on experiences from over-coming challenges in his personal and professional life. He has spoken on stages throughout North America and is known for mixing personal development into his technical presentations (e.g., guiding a room full of engineers through project-specific meditations).

Michael is passionate about empowering young professionals to become the Transcendent Leaders of tomorrow. His signature talk— *Bridging the gap between the generations in the workplace*—explores how each generation can better understand other generations, and how the differences between generations can be used to an organization's advantage.

Michael lives and breathes a high-performance lifestyle as an Ironman finisher, adventure athlete, and past member of the Canadian Youth Sailing Team.

For further information on corporate speaking engagements, live book performances, and for social media links to past talks, please connect with Michael through his website: michaeltranmer.com

Based in Vancouver, BC, Michael has found his dharma of living and creating his dream life while helping others do the same. *satori ananda* is his first book.